The Marion Library

Doorway to the future,
Picture window on the past

A look at Marion, Iowa, from
the city's most popular institution

Jean Strong

Ice Cube Press
North Liberty, Iowa

The Marion Library—Doorway to the future, Picture window on the past. A look at Marion, Iowa, from the city's most popular institution.

©2005 FRIENDS OF THE MARION, IOWA, PUBLIC LIBRARY
©2005 FRONT COVER BY BOB NAUJOKS
©2005 "Pioneering Ancestors" Jean Strong

ISBN 1-888160-03-9

First Edition

Library of Congress Control Number—2003105313

The paper used in this publication meets the minimum requirements of the American National Standard for Information Sciences—Permanence of Paper for Printed Library Materials, ANSI Z39.48-1992

Manufactured in the United States of America

Ice Cube Press
205 N. Front Street
North Liberty, Iowa 52317-9302
319/626-2055
icecube@inav.net
www.icecubepress.com

CONTENTS

FOREWORD

I am honored to be asked to write the Foreword for *The Marion Library* book. Having served as Marion City Council Member from 1970–1987 and Mayor from 1988–2003, I have been involved with several new city projects—the Police Station, Fire Station No. 2, Swimming Pool, Public Library and now the development of Lowe Park. I have watched the city grow and become a progressive community. The citizens of Marion have supported these projects and are to be commended.

I am especially proud of the Marion Public Library. This facility represents a remarkable public-private partnership. Literally hundreds of citizens were involved in planning, fund-raising and other facets of this project. I was involved from the start—space needs study, site selection, public forums, fund-raising, bond referendum that passed with a 74.3 percent approval rate, groundbreaking and grand opening. The library is very dear to my heart. I can't say enough about how it has become such a nucleus of the city. The new library has exceeded our expectations not only in appearance but more importantly in community reaction and patronage. It is a major part of our community. It is our "front door."

I would like to thank Jean Strong and Library Board Member Voanne Hansen for their dedication and commitment to this book. In addition, I would like to thank Library Director Susan Kling and the Library Board for all their help and support of this project, the Friends of the Marion Library for sponsoring the publication and, as well, I would like to thank the library staff who assisted with the collection of information.

The history of Marion is important to me. This publication is another way of preserving our heritage for future generations.

Victor L. Klopfenstein
Mayor of Marion,
1988-2003

TRIBUTE TO LIBRARY DIRECTOR SUSAN KLING

Susan Kling has played a major role in bringing library services in Marion into the 21st century.

Since 1905, when the Marion Carnegie Library opened, patrons had gone to the tile-roofed brick building at 13th Street and Seventh Avenue. Ms. Kling became the facility's director in May 1987 and soon realized that the city had outgrown its library.

She recommended in June of 1989 that the board of trustees begin planning for either enlargement or replacement of the building. The board commissioned a study to assess the community's library needs two to three decades into the future. With Ms. Kling's leadership, the board decided to build a new structure on a new site.

Though she never before had undertaken such a project, Ms. Kling worked through each step with trustees, city officials and others. She kept library services flowing smoothly all the while. The process included raising private funds, hiring consultants, choosing an architect and passing a bond issue. Many special people stepped in to help. Ms. Kling provided the leadership that kept everyone working together. Her manner and attitude made the project a positive experience.

Moving into the new building brought new challenges. The time-tested card catalog was retired in favor of a computerized circulation system. Staff had to be trained for new procedures. Inevitable new-building headaches abounded. Throughout it all, Ms. Kling kept everyone moving forward. The new Marion Public Library opened on July 22, 1996.

Marion's library became more popular and more of a community meeting place than ever before. Soon after moving to the new building, Ms. Kling began working with the Cedar Rapids Public Library on cooperative measures to improve efficiency and better serve patrons of the entire metro area.

Harry Baumert
President, Board of Trustees,
1989-2001

ACKNOWLEDGMENTS

The Marion Library book celebrates the 100th birthday of the Marion Library, 1905-2005, and aspires to be a valuable research tool in the future. Creating this book was an ambitious endeavor by a small group of dedicated individuals. A multitude of e-mails were exchanged among people associated with the Marion Library, the publisher in North Liberty, Iowa, and the author in northwest Arkansas. Diligent research—sifting through hundreds of collected photographs, information and anecdotes—turned up material that breathes life into history. The Book Committee accepts responsibility for any errors that slip through and holds blameless individuals and organizations we wish to acknowledge for valuable help.

We wish to thank:
Harry Baumert, library photos
Cedar Rapids Gazette, photos
Cindi Brown, research, copy editing, photos
French Studios, photo
Friends of the Marion Library, *The Marion Library* book sponsor
Sue Galvin, Bertha Owen photo
Hall's Photo, photos
Scott Hansen, photo collection
Voanne Hansen, photo collection
Bernice and Brent Harstad, photo
Nelda Y. Hoover, Kramer photo
Judy Hull, research, proofing, copy editing
Patricia Klopfenstein, photo collection
Marion Times, photos
Laurence Martin, Bill Reed photos
Bob Naujoks, front cover design
Steve Semken, library photos, back cover and book design.
Lynda Waddington, library board photo

THE BOOK COMMITTEE:
Molly Andersen
Voanne Hansen, head researcher
Irene Kincheloe
Susan Kling, Library Director
Nancy A. Miller
Jean Strong, editor and head writer

REFERENCES:
Cedar Rapids Gazette
Flying Tiger Website, www.danford.net
History of Marion, Iowa: a 20th Century Journey from Past to Present, researched & written by Marion High School students. 1998.
Judy Hull, Marion Swamp Fox Festival books:
  When the Railroad Came to Marion!, 1999
  The Merchants of Marion, 1840 to 2000, 2000
  A Walk Down Pucker Street, 2002
Marion City Directories
Marion Library Archives
Marion Sentinel
Marion Times
O.O.P. Club
Oak Shade Cemetery Burial Records
Oral histories: Lester DeWayne "Bud" Dickey, George Lowe and Ralph Mills.
Marvin Oxley, *History of Marion, Iowa*
Jean Strong, *A Prairie Almanac: 1839-1919*

LIBRARY REPORT AT 100

By Susan Kling,
Library Director
Marion Public Library

YOUR LIBRARY

In planning the new library, we took our time explaining our needs to the City Council and to the community. We looked at various sites, interviewed architects and hired a fund raising consultant. More than half of the cost of the new library came from private donations.

January 2004

When I started working at the Marion Public Library in January of 1987, I was impressed with the organization of the library and with the staff. It was my first experience in a public library. Previously, I worked at the Nebraska Library Commission in Lincoln, for 16 years. I left Nebraska in 1986 when my family moved to Cedar Rapids where my husband Bill accepted a job at Life Investors Insurance Company (Aegon).

The Library Board hired me as Director several months later after the former director resigned. Barb Ford, Marlys Maske, Barb Penn, and Jean Hampson—full-time employees at the library when I became the director—taught me a great deal about the library and our customers. I appreciated all their help and support.

Almost immediately, I realized that the library facility was extremely crowded: very little space for new books, hardly any electrical outlets for computers and only three off-street parking spaces. A one hundred thousand dollar bequest from the estate of Jeanne R. Bowdish in March 1989 provided the start of a solution. Interest income from that bequest was used to hire a consultant to do a space needs assessment.

The consultant's report offered several options including the one to build a new library with at least 22,000 square feet rather than try to expand the Carnegie library.

And so our building project began. It took seven years from start to finish. I have never been so busy in my life and I have never worked on a project that gave me so much satisfaction.

Our library is a busy place. On average, 875 people visit each day and check out more than 1600 items. Library programs for citizens of all ages are popular. We regularly schedule preschool story times each week as well as summer and winter reading programs for children, young adults and adults.

Because our community is growing faster than expected, we must think about expanding the facility. When the building expansion occurs, 19 parking spaces on the west side will be eliminated. Anticipating this, the Library Foundation in November of 2003 purchased property across the street (1101 Sixth Avenue, the old post office). Owning this property for future parking makes planning for expansion easier and our library users will find a parking place when they visit.

This community loves its library and appreciates the dedicated staff that makes customers feel welcome while helping them locate what they seek. The Library Board and staff work together in confirming what the community wants and needs. I believe that is one of the reasons we are such a heavily used library. We constantly monitor new trends and formats and incorporate them into the collection when appropriate.

Marion is a wonderful place to live and to work. We have excellent rapport with all city staff and the library benefits from their services and expertise. We believe more Marion citizens will find their library a fun place to visit in the years ahead.

Susan Kling

I'm glad that we did the fund raising; it got a lot of people involved in the project and they took ownership of it. People in the community really feel like this is their library.

Library circulation (the number of items taken home) during fiscal year 2003 totaled 562,867 or 1,655 items per day. That represents a 90% increase since the new library opened.

Only seven public libraries in Iowa had a higher circulation than Marion in fiscal year 2003 (July 1, 2002–June 30, 2003). They were: Ames, Cedar Rapids, Des Moines, Iowa City, Sioux City, Urbandale and West Des Moines. All of these cities boast larger populations than Marion.

The library is open 64 hours each week (61 during the summer when we close on Sunday). Nine full-time and 14 part-time employees keep things humming.

Our online computer catalog system, shared with the Cedar Rapids and Hiawatha public libraries, enables our users to browse catalogs at all three libraries. We call ourselves the Metro Library Network—one card works at all three libraries.

Surrounded by her family in this 2002 photo, Susan Kling stands behind the pastel painting by Marion artist Karen Hoyt that shows a father reading to his four daughters. On either side of Bill and Susan Kling at center are her son Ken and wife Deborah (left). At right, Susan's son Thom and her mother, Rose Schaefer. Bill and Susan commissioned the painting in memory of her father, Victor, who "always stressed the importance of reading and education. Books were always a part of our lives. My sisters and I will always cherish the memory of his reading to us." The painting hangs in the children's area.

BENEVOLENT BENEFACTORS

Andrew Carnegie (1835-1919) provided $10,000 for constructing Marion's first library building, later granting an additional $1,500. The philanthropist Scotsman founded the forerunner of U.S. Steel. He provided construction funds for 101 libraries in Iowa.

Nancy A. Miller, a Cedar Rapids teacher, assured the success of a fund drive for the new Marion library with her pledge for $650,000 over five years.

Marion citizens have supported their library through the years, but special notice is owed to two benefactors who made the facilities possible. Andrew Carnegie amassed a fortune in the late 1800s selling bonds for financing railroad construction and steel rails to build the nationwide network that crossed Iowa. He responded to letters from Marion residents with an $11,500 gift for the town's first free public library in 1905. Teacher Nancy A. Miller, who had been using Marion's Carnegie Library as a teaching resource and for her own children (now adults), opted to share an inheritance to make the new Marion Library building seem possible in 1994. Her parents, Upton and Scottie Ziesler, owned and operated a home furnishings store in Manitowoc, Wisconsin, where Nancy was born in 1943.

The legacy her parents wanted to pass on to Nancy and her sister was threefold: religion, education and travel. Nancy is a 1965 graduate of Marquette University, Milwaukee, with a degree in Elementary Education and has taught school in some capacity ever since. Nancy came to Iowa in 1978, married Stephen Miller in 1982 and received an inheritance from her mother (also a former teacher) in 1993. In recognition of her gift, the building bears Nancy's name. "I'm just an ordinary person," Nancy responded to questions about her generous act; she "saw the value of reading, books and libraries" and hopes "the children I taught, neighborhood children and my own children will see that I made this financial commitment because I believe so strongly in education and reading. My donation is a legacy to all children that I have known or will ever know."

Mr. Carnegie (1835-1919) was born in Scotland, son of a weaver displaced by the Industrial Revolution. At age 12, he emigrated with his parents to Pittsburgh, Pennsylvania. As a young man on his way up, Carnegie had access to a library for working boys that "opened the intellectual wealth of the world to me," he later remarked. More than 2800 libraries were built as a result of his largesse; he became "the father of modern philanthropy" by giving away 90 percent of his $350-million fortune.

'Bravo' to these two philanthropists for their generous gifts to the Marion community.

First Library 1905-1996

Originating in the Industrial Age, Marion's first library struggled for operating funds from the beginning. The Marion Federation of Women's Clubs purchased the adjoining lot to the west and continued supporting the library for many years. The building was remodeled several times and enlarged once.

After serving as Marion's library for 91 years, the Carnegie building was placed on the National Register of Historic Places. The photo above, courtesy of Bernice and Brent Harstad, depicts the Carnegie library as it looked during the winter of 1959-60. In 1996, the Methodist church purchased the building.

The Library Corner

The corner lot on Seventh Ave. at 13th St. cost $3,973. Architects Dieman & Fiske designed the building; construction began in September 1904 under contract for $9,898 with A.H. Conners. In 1916, the Marion Federation of Women's Clubs purchased the lot west of the library to enlarge the grounds.

New Library takes shape
Between May 1987—July 1996

Nine years after the Library Board hired Susan Kling as library director, the new library building opened south of City Square Park. The site was among two dozen considered by the site committee. Fund-raiser George Lowe said: "The building itself came in under contract, the location made the project community-based and town-centered, the fund drive was brief and the spirit in which all of the participants worked commendable." Major players in the accomplishment were the Library Board, the City Council, community leaders and volunteers, donors and the voting citizens of Marion.

BUDGET FOR THE NEW LIBRARY

Site acquisition	**$683,000**
Demolition	**129,240**
Construction	**2,976,669**
Furniture/furnishings	**570,000**
Professional fees, misc.	**20,058**
Total budget	**$4,378,967**

The Marion Public Library since 1996 provides more services for a growing population. A Cedar Rapids teacher and her husband were major donors for the new library building. Their pledge in 1994 assured the success of a fund drive before Marion citizens voted for the bond issue that provided $1,975,000 toward the needed funds (Photo by French Studios).

Nancy A. and Stephen Miller

INVOLVING COMMUNITY

Gearing up to attract new library patrons and offer opportunities for participation began in May 1989 with an organizational meeting for Friends of the Library. The group now has more than 300 members. In 1996, events were held in the lobby and auditorium to attract new patrons and provide entertainment.

The Red Cedar Chamber Music duo of John Dowdall and Jan Boland (above) attracted a crowd (below) to several chamber music events held in the lobby of the new library.

Friends of the Marion Library and Its Foundation

Community Support
1989-2004 History
By Voanne Hansen and
Susan Kling

In the 15 years of its existence, Friends of the Marion Library have become valued partners. The group was organized on 6 May 1989, by the steering committee, chaired by Bettymae Ketelsen (Airy); with the assistance of Llewellyn "Boo" Balster, library board member, and Susan Kling, library director. Forty-two members had enrolled and six hundred

LIBRARY FOUNDATION COMMITTEE

At right, the Library Foundation Committee in spring 2004 includes, left to right, back row: Russ Miller, Paul Orcutt, Bettymae Airy, Pat Klopfenstein, Clair Lensing, Leigh Enneking, Gerry Eganhouse, John Vernon, Bob Buckley (library board president); middle: Nancy A. Miller, Sara Fishel (committee president), Jim Bouslog (treasurer); front: Susan Kling (library director) and Cindy Nielsen. Not included in photo: Sue Katz and Mike Tibor.

THE FRIENDS BOARD OF DIRECTORS, SPRING 2004
Front row, l to r: Pat Kress, secretary; Pat Otis, Marlys Claussen, Kay McGuire, Karen Roltgen. Back row, l to r: Paula Pearson; Marcia Myers, president; Trudy Stenersen; Chuck Boquist; Sara Dostal; Sue Verhille and Susie Dale. Board members not pictured: Lori Lane Klopfenstein, Mark Klopfenstein, Tina Monroe, vice-president, and Lowell Morgan.

and five dollars were ready for deposit in a bank account. First board members were Bob Buckley, Theresa Riley, Dick Snyder, Karen Alderson, Marjorie Reynolds, Jeanne Strothman, Kay McGuire, Margaret McLaughlin and John Vernon.

Organized as a nonprofit citizens' group that "believed in the importance of library services and cultural activities connected with the library," the Friends set first-year goals. To provide extra funding for the library, they held two book sale events, sponsored a variety of programs in the library, acted as advocate for the library by raising city council awareness of the need for additional programs and informing the community of services provided. Supporting these aims, they produce a newsletter and host a dinner meeting with a well-known author as speaker.

When the new building was in its planning stage, the Friends requested a room in the facility to store books for future sales. A small space off the lobby was designated for this purpose. Those early plans for storage evolved into a more ambitious goal: a used-book store. The store opened 1 November 1996 with an all-volunteer staff, shelving, a desk, chair and file and a small collection of materials. Under leadership of Marilyn Phelps, the first store manager, a philosophy and structure were established for operating the store 36 hours a week. Quality merchandise would be offered and each item individually priced. Most of the stock came, then as now, from public contributions with a small amount from library deletions. The store stocks the best of the contributions; other gifts are set aside for semiannual book sales. Store sales add about $18,000 a year to the Friends' budget and book sales add another $3,500. In 2003, the Friends contributed $12,500 toward the purchase of the lot for additional patron parking across 11th Street.

In 2004, the Friends paid for the creation and publication of *The Marion Library* book you hold in your hands. In addition to its historical perspective, the book includes, as its final section, a pictorial presentation of services available in the new library.

The Marion Public Library Foundation was established to provide long-term financial support to enhance the services and collections of the library— *both today and tomorrow.*

Since 1996, the Foundation's endowment from Sue and Bert Katz has financially supported the library's summer reading programs for children and young adults.

A 2002 donation from the Henry and Sara Katz Charitable Foundation provided $25,000 for purchasing children's library materials.

In November of 2003, the Foundation purchased the former Marion post office property across 11th Street from the library. The land will be used for future library parking.

Bob Buckley speaks at organizational meeting for Friends of the Marion Library in May 1989.

Patrons will remember the front desk of the Carnegie Library as it was in 1996 before the library was moved to the new building (Photo by Hall's).

In the new library, patrons line up at the checkout desk. Other tasks performed by checkout people: issue new library cards, send and receive faxes, continuously empty the book return bins, check in returned materials and place on carts for sorting and reshelving. (Photo by Harry Baumert)

DEMOLITION & CONSTRUCTION 1994-1996

Library site, bordered by 6th and 5th avenues and 10th and 11th streets, before demolition began in late December 1994.

Library Director Susan Kling, (3rd from right) and Board President Harry Baumert (4th from right) wield shovels to break ground on a rainy spring day in 1995.

Construction began in August 1995.

Opening Day—22 July 1996

Community Leader George Lowe and Director Susan Kling (left) share a congratulatory hug at the ribbon cutting ceremony. American Legion members (right) conduct flag raising ceremony.

At Grand Opening on 24 August, State Librarian Sharman Smith addresses the gathering outside the Library.

On opening day, breakfast is served and sponsored by McDonald's and WMT-AM Radio at the Pavilion in City Square Park. Lunch was served and sponsored by Burger King and WMT-FM Radio.

MARION LIBRARY BOARD OF TRUSTEES, 2004

A nine-member Board of Trustees governs the library. Trustee responsibilities include hiring the Library Director, setting policy, making financial decisions and working with the director to ensure quality library service. Members are appointed by the Mayor and approved by the City Council. The Trustees meet monthly and serve six-year terms. Harry Baumert resigned from the Board and Kevin Gertsen was appointed for a six-year-term beginning 1 July 2004.

Front row (from left): Eileen Robinson, secretary; Voanne Hansen; Bob Buckley, president; Molly Andersen, vice-president; Irene Kincheloe. Back row from left: Linda Wilson, Harry Baumert, Jack Zumwalt and Nancy A. Miller, honorary board member. Sally Reck (lower left inset).

WHAT MAKES MARION SPECIAL?

WHAT DO
YOU THINK?

HINT: THE EYE
OF THE BEHOLDER

Easterners and southerners alike came to the beautiful Iowa prairie in Linn County in the late 1830s. Each man chose the spot he fancied. At a dollar twenty-five an acre, the land—with its fertile soil, ample trees and water—was a bargain. Among Linn County's first four settlements, Marion, Iowa, alone survives in the 21st century. Ivanhoe and Westport (both organized in 1838 along the north bank of the Cedar River in Franklin and Bertram townships), disappeared years ago as their fortunes shifted, and Columbus (September 1838) became part of west Cedar Rapids following three name changes—Columbus to Kingston to Rapids City and finally to Cedar Rapids in 1841.

From April 1839 onward, Marion's identity was never in doubt. Named to honor a Revolutionary War general, Marion was found ideal as the county seat because of its strategic location near the county's center. A horse thief named Osgood Shepard was the first settler in what became Cedar Rapids while a man from Vermont (Luman M. Strong) chose Marion in 1839 and was elected as one of three county commissioners (called supervisors since 1872). As federal law required, the free state of Iowa was paired with a slave state (Texas) when it gained statehood in 1846.

Marion area citizens embraced the sentiment of the state motto: "Our liberties we prize and our rights we will maintain," and extended the idea to friendly Native Americans who were here before the white men came. Linn County residents petitioned state and federal governments requesting that the natives be allowed to purchase land along the Iowa River rather than be relocated to a government reservation. The Meskwaki Indian Settlement in Tama County was the result.

Mindful of their patriotic duty, menfolk from Linn County volunteered for military service. A promising young Marion businessman died in the Mexican War (1846-1848); William H. Woodbridge had built Marion's first brick house and helped to establish Marion's first store (Woodbridge and Thompson). Thomas Jefferson McKean, a West Point graduate, trained a squad in Marion to fight in that same war, and 15 years later voluntarily served as an officer in the Civil War (1861-1865). On returning home he was elected Marion's first mayor. More than 40 other men have followed in that office since and several displayed exceptional leadership skills.

Some veterans returned to Marion from the war-ravaged southern states to help their home city prosper. To be sure there were hardships, but none as great as those endured by southerners whose homes and lands were the battlefields during four years of the bitter civil strife. Marion businesses and local government gradually provided a safe water system, efficient fire fighting and law enforcement. Progress came on the heels of technological innovation but another 15 years went by following the Civil War before an interurban street railway offered public transportation between Marion and Cedar Rapids. That service began in April 1880.

In the 1900s, U.S. Highway 30 accommodates automobiles on the Marion Boulevard between Marion and Cedar Rapids. Interurban rail tracks ran along the south side. The stretch of road was paved after the 1919 court house election.

Marion grew faster than Cedar Rapids until 1870 and prevailed for 86 years as the seat of county government; but the voting citizens in Rapids Township finally outnumbered those in Marion and eastern townships that favored Marion over the more distant city. Cedar Rapids won the courthouse by ballot in 1919 following 64 years of contention. Another four years passed before a majority of county voters approved the bond issue for building a new courthouse on May's Island in the Cedar River in 1923. It was completed in 1925.

In 1926 the Board of County Supervisors passed resolutions granting the park property opposite the former courthouse to the city of Marion provided it always be "used exclusively for park purposes." Marion city officials won the bid at public auction to purchase the old courthouse itself for twelve hundred dollars but failed to complete the deal because funds were not obtainable.

A dam on Indian Creek created power for Marion's small saw and flour mills. A larger dam on the Cedar gave Cedar Rapids superior water power to expand its industrial base and surpass Marion in industrial importance before the 1900s.

A public water fountain replaced the town pump and its community cup in City Square Park during J.C. Davis' final years as mayor and provided a tasty, cold, spring-water drink for man, woman and child—especially appreciated on warm summer nights when the school band offered concerts in the park. Cedar Rapids' residents filled their jugs with the spring water when their own water supply became malodorous. Cedar Rapids won the race for train service in 1859, but trains steamed into Marion five years later, in October 1864.

The local trains provided transportation between towns for athletic teams and other commuters—an alternative to travel by horse and buggy or wagons in the late 1880s. Many trees were felled to provide fuel for the engines.

When a switching center and roundhouse for the Chicago, Milwaukee, St. Paul and Pacific Railroad was developed in 1881, on the east edge of town, Marion became an important railroad town. The railroad created jobs and for a time was Marion's largest employer. The railroad history was remembered in the 1990s by architects who used a railroad motif in designing the new public library building. The roof and bricks from the old depot serve as a pavilion in City Square Park. Paving projects gradually lifted Marion's city streets out of the gummy mud and frozen ruts well before the first automobiles arrived in the early 1900s.

Around the turn of the century, events hastened further change. "The gas plant north of Iowa's first enduring national bank supplied gas for the gas lights in town before the plant exploded

THE MILL DAM, AND TOOGOOD'S HILL.

East Star Mill (above) on Indian Creek was established in the 1860s, purchased in 1881 by A. Howeler who sold it to his sons in 1908.

One of the Numerous Springs

Pure spring water was the source of the city supply for Marion from 1886 to 1952. A spring house covers the spring along Indian Creek.

in 1894," Carrie Davis Reichert recalled. In 1903 home owners scurried to affix numbers to their homes before free mail delivery service began early in 1904, and 21 letter boxes were installed around business and residential areas north and south of Sixth Avenue to facilitate outgoing mail collection.

In 1905, electricity began to light city streets. The main road to the west that some called "the most beautiful drive in eastern Iowa" was named Marion Boulevard. Thomas Park, with its picnicking facilities, was promoted in the 1920s as a tourist rest stop for intercontinental travelers along this stretch of the Lincoln Highway (U.S. 30). Downtown Mom and Pop grocery stores slowly gave way to supermarkets mid-way into the 20th century as Marion's business district began expanding eastward along Seventh Avenue.

Railroad yards east of downtown accommodated rail traffic on the Chicago, Milwaukee, St. Paul and Pacific Railroad from 1881 until 1918 when the division point and roundhouse were moved to Atkins. Freight service continued until February 1980.

By the 1960s, Marion was eastern Iowa's fastest growing city due partly to employment opportunities at Collins Radio (now Rockwell Collins) in northeast Cedar Rapids, and desirable housing nearby. In 1960, Marion's population reached 10,882 residents, surpassed 18,000 in 1970 and grew to more than 26,000 by 2000.

So what makes Marion special? The people, of course; those who planned and those who worked to assure that the city would maintain its small-town charm as it grew. A lot of hard work by thousands of people has made Marion an attractive residential city designed for gracious living in the 21st century.

Sun Mart Supermarket in the east end was the first of the big grocery stores to emerge. Henry Katz, a native of Marion, began development to the east of downtown in the 1950s.

Luman Mastin Strong arrived in March 1839 and built the first home in Marion near Indian Creek, south of "Short Street," known today as Central Avenue. Then 35, he had come from Vermont by way of Springfield, Ohio, where his first wife died, and Davenport, Iowa, where he married his second wife. After numerous businessmen slept on the floor of the Strong home, Luman expanded it into an inn and welcomed the newcomers.

Luman Strong had been appointed a justice of the peace by the Territorial Government at Burlington and Marion's first postmaster by President Martin Van Buren's postmaster-general. He was elected a Linn County Commissioner and as first inn keeper was granted the county's first liquor license.

Strong's chosen claim, some 165 acres, extended north along the creek and east to the Owen Block that was to be developed downtown north of City Square Park. He purchased his land from Addison Daniels, Marion merchant and land speculator, who arrived in 1840 from Massachusetts with money to invest.

Historian Marvin Oxley described the Strong Inn in his *History of Marion, Iowa*. Although built of hewn logs, he wrote, it was "finished up on the outside like a frame house, and had an upper and lower porch facing town. There was nothing else so elaborate in central Iowa in 1840." Strong had hauled materials (lumber, glass and nails) for the inn from Rock Island, Illinois.

By 1874, when Orville Strong (1843-1931) from Wisconsin visited family and friends in the Marion area, he reported in a letter to his mother in Dodgeville that Marion's first house, his birthplace, was "sadly dilapidated" and that "a few years more will number it among the things that were."

As one of the first three county commissioners (now called supervisors), Vermont native Luman Strong helped Linn County government get underway. [The other two commissioners were Samuel C. Stewart from Linn Township and Peter McRoberts of Ivanhoe in Franklin Township.] Luman located Marion's cemetery south of the business area in a hilly section with many trees, aptly named Oak Shade. His first two Iowa-born babies are buried there in unmarked graves.

Strong was one of three men who represented Linn County at the First Iowa Constitutional Convention in 1844. The other two were Samuel W. Durham and Thomas J. McKean. A second

PIONEERING ANCESTORS

BY GREAT-GREAT-GRANDAUGHTER JEAN STRONG

Luman M. Strong (1803-1867)

"Marion is the prettiest town I have seen in my travels though there are other points which are better for business."
—Orville Strong, 1874

convention two years later succeeded in extending the state's western boundary to the Missouri River and achieved statehood for Iowa in 1846.

In 1848, Strong and his family (second wife Mary Gabbert, a Virginian teaching in Davenport before her marriage, and their five-year-old son Orville) moved north to the Territory of Wisconsin. Several children from Luman's first marriage (wife, Nancy Griswold of Vermont) went with them, but Luman's youngest son, Henry G. Strong, had remained in Ohio after his 35-year-old mother died. Henry was an infant of one year and his father presumably left him with neighbors as had happened to Luman when he was orphaned as an infant in Vermont.

After reaching his majority, Henry Strong came to Iowa in 1856. He later married Christina Lutz, daughter of another Linn County pioneer family, and they raised their family of four on farms, the last one located north of Marion near Alburnett.

In the early 1900s, Henry's youngest son, George A. Strong, bought 199 acres from the Benjamin Bowman Estate located one mile northwest of Marion on the Alburnett Road. He had married one of Bowman's daughters, Nettie (1869-1914), and they had two sons, Dale Bowman Strong (1897-1949) and Walter Benjamin Strong (1901-1951), the author's father.

In Wisconsin, Luman Strong was fortunate in having a reliable team of horses that allowed him to 'read the law' while hauling ore from the lead mines in Highland, Wisconsin, to Galena, Illinois. His horses knew the way. After being admitted to the Wisconsin bar, Luman was elected to the Wisconsin legislature and then three times as Iowa County judge in Dodgeville where he built a substantial brick home in 1865—two years before he died. Orville built his home next door to his parents.

Luman was proud of being a popular Democrat in a Republican area, and of his son, Orville Strong, who had served in the Civil War and later established the Strong Bank (1881-1981) in Dodgeville. Another son, Amanzer, from the first marriage, also fought in the Civil War.

Luman Strong had helped organize the Democratic Party in Linn County and was the first inductee into Marion's Masonic Lodge #6. His great disappointment in life, due to failing health, was that he did not achieve the top Masonic rank in

NOTES ABOUT THE STRONGS:

Luman's son, Henry (1835-1915), and grandson, George (1870-1936), rest in Marion's Oak Shade Cemetery.

George A. Strong in 1912 used a plan similar to the 1909 home of James and Ida Bowman for his farm home on Alburnett Road. The Bowman home is one of those on the National Register of Historic Places on Pucker Street.

In December 1916, George Strong sold access rights and a fraction of an acre along a spring-fed creek for one dollar to the Marion Water Company. Strong's father-in-law, Benjamin Bowman, and Attorney J.C. Davis had granted permission for using springs on their properties for city water decades earlier.

In 1939, Adolph Boyson, Cedar Rapids jeweler, purchased the Bowman-Strong farm (from the George A. Strong Estate). Widow Ida had moved to Marion. Son Dale moved to Cedar Rapids in 1936 and worked for the railroad; son Walter and family moved to a farm they purchased south of Springville in January 1940.

Amanzer Strong (1832-1915), school teacher who was a 1st Lieutenant in the Civil War, and his older brother, Orrin (in produce), owned property at one time in Rapids Township, Linn County, but settled elsewhere in Iowa.

the Wisconsin lodge. His will did not mention two surviving daughters or son Henry by name, but he left five dollars to each of them. Henry was 32 and living in Iowa. Daughter Emily (Mrs. Charles C. Cook) lived in Cedar Rapids after her marriage.

In the early 2000s, descendants of Luman's Iowa family planted a flowering tree near Strong's gravesite in the East Side Cemetery at Dodgeville. In his will, Strong had asked to be buried "under a native tree where the birds can sing my requiem." The original native tree shading his grave had succumbed to the elements. The stone marker near the tree identifies Judge Strong as "Marion, Iowa pioneer 1839-1848."

The Marion Historical Society restored a home on 10th Street at Central Avenue that is open to visitors. Called Granger House, it was built on land formerly claimed by Luman Strong. The society's second project was the Marion Heritage Center, established in 2000 in the former First Baptist Church across 10th St. from the new library.

Isaac N. Kramer
(1832-1923)
Nurseryman and author

General Thomas J. McKean
(1810-1870)

An 1831 graduate of West Point, New York, T.J. McKean was born in Bradford County, Pennsylvania. He had a keen sense of public duty. He resigned his army commission in 1834 to become a civil engineer; moved to Marion in 1840; married Sarah P. Gray in 1848; three children. He served two terms as county surveyor. He resigned as county sheriff in 1861 to fight in the Civil War; commanded the Sixth Army Division at Corinth, Mississippi, 4-5 October 1862. On his return to Marion, he was elected the city's first mayor in 1865.

Samuel W. Durham
(1817-1909)
Surveyor, land owner
& story teller

Isaac N. Kramer left as his legacy an unedited book manuscript describing the early history of Linn County, published in 1996 as *A Prairie Almanac: 1839 to 1919*. He came to Iowa with his family by river from New Geneva, Pennsylvania, in 1839 when he was 7. Later he built the county's first greenhouse, operated a nursery and seed business on the Boulevard west of Indian Creek and, with his son Judson, maintained a retail outlet in Cedar Rapids. Isaac's daughter, Adelaide, worked at the Marion site. Daughter Ella (Mrs. Frank Lund) lived in Alexandria, Virginia, in 1923.

Soldier, engineer,
surveyor, sheriff & mayor

Samuel Durham, descendant of a Kentucky pioneer family, lived a long life with near-total recall. "All (three of the) first county officers, after seeing Iowa well established, (went) to other newer countries, not waiting to reap the full fruits of their labors here," he said. Durham came to Iowa on horseback in 1840 from Vallonia, Indiana. He surveyed large portions of north and northwestern Iowa and Minnesota. His wife, Ellen Wolcott, came to Iowa from New York with her mother and sister Mary (Mrs. William Abbe). Ellen taught school in Marion in 1843. Luman Strong married the young couple.

'Swell' Homes and People
on 'Pucker Street' and Elsewhere

The "refined ladies living along fashionable Pucker Street objected to the noise" made on brick pavement by the hooves of horses. In 1901, they succeeded in getting the town's first asphalt paving from 12th to 22nd streets years before automobiles even appeared. Eighth Avenue was dubbed 'Pucker Street' because of the 'swells' that lived on it in the early days. In fairness to all taxpayers, more than half of the $23,000 paving cost was assessed against properties along that section of avenue.

Pioneer merchant Amory Keyes and his wife brought four daughters to Marion from the East in the 1840s. The daughters married young business and professional men who became successful. One of the younger daughters, Helen Keyes (Mrs. James) Giffen, set the pattern for the "subdued but gracious social life" for Marion; her husband was an attorney from Pennsylvania. The other daughters were Mary Ann (Mrs. Preston Daniels); Caroline (Mrs. Thomas Downing) and Eliza (Mrs. Robert Holmes).

Other prominent families who built and/or lived in fine homes on Pucker were bank presidents Jeremiah S. Alexander and James Bowman; lumberman Tuiller J. Davis; grocer Benjamin F. Mentzer and druggists Thomas R. Alexander, George Miller and Carl N. Owen.

Two notable homes not on 'Pucker Street' should be mentioned. The octagon house on Fourth Avenue at 9th Street was built in the 1800s by Major J.B. Young. The other, on 13th Street is known as the Waffle House. Mrs. Waffle said the home, built in the late 1890s, had the first water closet

Stylish women on 6th Avenue adorn a 1908 post card. Musician Kit Burroughs (front) played piano for silent films. Her mother had a hat shop on 7th Avenue before the 1894 fire.

The Preston Daniels family lived in the 1853 home he built on 8th Ave. at 13th St. Daughter Adeliza Daniels continued living here until the late 1940s.

(indoor toilet) in Marion. Historian Marvin Oxley lived on the second floor. The Waffles were long-time booksellers in Marion.

J.S. Alexander lived at 1375 8th Ave. The Civil War veteran retired from the lumber business in 1891, served as bank president and state senator. Benjamin Mentzer, son of a building contractor, built home at right in the 1890s.

Tuillar J. and Nellie Davis purchased this home in the 1600 block of 8th Ave. in 1901 and sold it in 1918. A Marion landmark from the 1800s, the home is no longer standing.

In 1910, Merle and his horse-drawn wagon may have made deliveries to Pucker Street ladies who took exception to the noise horses' hooves made on brick paving.

PEOPLE MAKING THE DIFFERENCE

The following people were chosen to represent the hundreds who have made a difference in Marion. Jacob C. Davis, an attorney with civic pride in the late 1800s, and Veterinarian Victor Klopfenstein bookend this group of loyal supporters of the Library.

J.C. "JAKE" DAVIS, 66 YEARS, 1843-1909

Attorney Jake Davis was progressive with a sense of history. He installed the first telephones from his law office to the courthouse. With Mr. Beall, he organized the first meeting of Old Settlers in 1891 and in 1898 bought the first auto. He also bought the first typewriter but discarded it when he learned "it couldn't spell." His daughter, Carrie Davis (Mrs. Carl) Reichert, wrote about him in the late 1950s. He converted the historic Presbyterian church (610 10th Street) into a law office and home in which his family lived. [In 2004, it houses an insurance agency and an investment counselor.] German-born Davis served as mayor for nine one-year terms in 1871-1874, 1876 and 1886-1889. Beginning in 1896, elections were held every two years. He died at age 66. Carrie lived from 1874 to 1963 and was a loyal Marion supporter. Remembering the time when it was true, she wrote: "I always call Cedar Rapids a suburb of Marion."

ADELIZA DANIELS, 93 YEARS, 1854-1947

Miss Adeliza Daniels, daughter of a distinguished pioneer family, spearheaded the drive for a public library building in Marion early in the 1900s. Her father, Preston Daniels, came to Marion in 1846 from Massachusetts. Adeliza is credited with being the single most important person in bringing about the Carnegie Library (as Nancy A. Miller was vital to obtaining funding for the second library building in 1994). Miss Daniels was chief organizer and president of the Marion Federation of Women's Clubs for 11 years. One of the original members of the Library Board of Trustees, she soon resigned to devote her time to assuring the library's survival. Adeliza and others wrote Andrew Carnegie asking for $10,000 toward the building fund plus another $1,500 toward the site purchase at 13th Street. Carnegie's philanthropic organization required that the city provide a two-mill tax rate

Mayor Jake Davis

Daughter Carrie Reichert

Miss Adeliza Daniels

29

annually for maintenance. Her father, Preston, and bachelor uncle, Addison Daniels, were early Marion entrepreneurs. Adeliza lived to 93.

BERTHA LEE OWEN, 71 YEARS, 1866-1937

Bertha Lee Lake of Marengo married the young Marion pharmacist, Carl N. Owen, in 1889 and "found time aside from her home duties all through the years to aid her husband as bookkeeper at the store. She was keen of mind, not afraid to express opinions on matters of concern and was ever true to her ideals." Two of the Owens' four children grew to adulthood. Mrs. Owen's "energy and enthusiasm" for work with the Marion Federation of Women's Clubs helped realize Marion's first library building in 1905; until her death she served on the Library Board of Trustees. Mrs. Owen was an active member in the Congregational Church; Chapter 183, Order of the Eastern Star; Lorraine Circle of Past Matrons; Entre Nous Club and charter member of Marion-Linn Chapter, Daughters of the American Revolution. She died at 71.

Bertha Lake Owen (Mrs. Carl) served on the Marion Library Board, 1903-1937. Her daughter, Norma Owen Howell, was appointed to fill her position upon Mrs. Owen's death.

MARVIN OXLEY, 86 YEARS, 1883-1969

Marvin Oxley will be long remembered for compiling five volumes of Marion history and rare photographs. The original volumes, preserved at the Marion Library, have been a valuable resource for this book as well as earlier books about the city and its people. In the 1940s, Mr. Oxley was Marion Parks Commissioner. A longtime member of the Library Board of Trustees, Oxley was killed in an auto mishap in 1969 at the intersection of Eighth Avenue and 13th Street as he walked to the library. He was 86.

EMERY J. MILLER, 87 YEARS, 1885-1972

Emery Miller served on the Library Board for 44 years—1926-1970—until a young new mayor replaced him with his own choice. Miller's abilities and involvement in business and community affairs suited him as board president for many of those years. Ralph Mills, retired city engineer whose wife, the late Ruth Mills, worked as library director, told interviewers, "Emery Miller, the banker, was an excellent man." Born in Pulaski, Iowa, 26 June 1885, Miller died in Marion 1 November 1972. He was 87. He

Marvin Oxley was honored with a plaque for his ambitious five-volume *History of Marion, 1838-1927*.

had served on the First National Bank board, as board chairman and bank president; past president of the Linn County Bankers Association, charter member of the Marion Evening Lions, secretary of the Marion Independent School board, director and former secretary of the Marion Masonic Association, 50-year member and past master of the Marion Lodge No. 6, AF & AM and member and senior warden emeritus of St. John's Episcopal Church in Cedar Rapids; his only son, John, died in WW II.

Emery Miller

HENRY AND BERT KATZ FAMILIES

Henry Katz and his brother Bert, Marion natives, worked side by side as owners of Katz Salvage and Auto Parts for 45 years (sold in 1985); they owned the Marion Mobile Home Park until December 1999. Henry "was truly dedicated to the growth and enhancement of Marion." He and his brother donated parcels of land to the city for the new police and fire stations. Both are major supporters of the Marion Library. Sara, Henry's wife of 58 years, died in 2000; he died in 2001 at age 90. Bert chairs the Henry and Sara Katz Charitable Foundation. Funds from this Foundation and a personal gift from Bert and his wife Suzanne "Sue" Katz were instrumental in securing the post office property on Sixth Avenue as a future parking lot for the library. Sue and Bert established an endowment fund in the Library Foundation, funding the children's summer reading programs at the library since 1997; Sue donated a bronze statue in memory of her son (See Section Four). Sue and Bert served as Grand Marshals of the Swamp Fox Parade in 2000.

Sara and Henry Katz

Sue and Bert Katz

GEORGE LOWE, 77 YEARS, 1925-2002

George Lowe came to the Marion area from Slayton, Minnesota, at age two. After serving in WWII, he married Alyce Bendix and took over his father's construction company that same year at age 21. He expanded the business to include eight other companies related to highway construction and retired from the crushed stone business in the 1980s. Although the Lowes never lived within the city limits, they were granted honorary citizenship by Mayor Vic Klopfenstein on behalf of the Marion city council in August 2000. Both Lowes served as Grand Marshals of the annual Swamp Fox Parade in 2001. During his term as president

George was intrumental in organizing the Marion Economic Development Corporation (MEDCO). Active in numerous organizations in Marion and Cedar Rapids, he led the Capital Fund-raising Campaign for the new Marion public library; in 2000 he and Alyce donated 182 acres of farmland to be developed as a community park. "The Lowes have made a number of wonderful financial contributions over the years," wrote *Marion Times* Editor Andrea Geddes in 2001, but even more impressive are the "hours and hours of donated time, the sharing of new ideas, door to door fundraising efforts and working alongside other community members to help Marion grow and prosper." About Lowe's death, Mayor Klopfenstein said, "We lost a giant of a man. We will certainly miss him and his driving force in the community." He was 77 when he died.

George Lowe

VICTOR KLOPFENSTEIN, CITY OFFICIAL, 1970-2003

Vic Klopfenstein is known for his devotion and hard work to make Marion a better place than he found it. After graduating from Iowa State University in 1962, he was recruited by Marion veterinarians Herman Strader and Al Evenson to join them as a partner of the Linn Animal Hospital. They moved their practice from a home location to the Marion Boulevard site. Born in rural Washington, Iowa, Vic's education was interrupted by army service and work on his father's turkey farm, but he received his first college degree in 1958. Eleven years later (1969), he and a slate of "mostly young businessmen" were elected to the city council pledging to bring a more professional approach to city operations. In 1988, he was elected mayor and served 16 years in that office. Acknowledging that team work was the key, his goals included the economic development of Marion, revitalization of the central business district, increased government efficiency, enhanced community identity and the new library building. After retiring from veterinary practice on 31 August 1998, Vic received the American Hometown Leaders Award from the WalMart Foundation. He was nominated by community residents who believed he "made a difference in the community." In the 2003 annual Swamp Fox parade, the Mayor and his wife, Pat, (who has worked beside him through the years) were honored as Grand Marshals.

Vic Klopenstein, former Mayor

CHANGE IS RELENTLESS

"My town is built around
        the square,
Surveyed in early days
By strong and hardy pioneers
Whose children live to give
        them praise.
Many old trees adorn the square,
Great elms and lofty maples too,
And one lone sycamore.
From the four corners
        walks are laid,
Which at a fountain meet.
Here tin cups hung in former days
The thirsty ones to greet.
Nobody knows how many
        germs met there in
        competition;
But sanitary fountains now give
        aid to germ depletion.
A bandstand by the fountain
Serves in a double way;
It seats the band on summer nights
And those who speak Old
        Settlers' day.
        —*Mabel Alexander,*
"My Town" book of poems, 1940.

Railroad tracks run between City Square Park (left) and the Linn County Courthouse at right in this 1910 photo. In 1996, the new library opened on the courthouse block site.

CITY SQUARE PARK

Marion's downtown square was the focal point for county business and community activities from the earliest days. Streets on the north and the south were thoroughfares for east-west travel. Seventh Avenue became U.S. Highway 30 and then 151. Sixth Avenue on the south, between City Square Park and the courthouse, accommodated horses first, then trains and finally shared the space with trains, autos and pedestrians. After the new Linn County Courthouse was completed at Cedar Rapids in 1925, the county supervisors deeded the park property to the City of Marion with the proviso that it always be a park as established in the original town plat. In the 21st century, the new library building occupies the full block south of City Square Park that continues to be a popular site for community activities.

"Every community requires certain character institutions that determine its community priorities. These include churches, libraries, schools and hospitals. If you look around the town center of Marion, you'll find three of those institutions are handy to the town center."—
George Lowe, interview with Nancy A. Miller, 19 April 2001

(left) This 1868 drawing shows a corner of City Square with tree plantings (top right corner) and buildings across 6th Ave. The second courthouse served from 1846 to 1925. Since 1996, the new Marion Public Library occupies the entire block between 5th and 6th avenues, 10th and 11th streets.

"Pegleg Rose"

Mabel Alexander wrote about one of the town characters called 'Pegleg Rose.' He was a signalman who "fell under a moving train." Miss Alexander's father, a druggist, and uncle, a doctor, amputated Bob Rose's leg that day without a nurse or anesthesiologist in attendance, and no hospital in town. "They took it as part of the day's work and Bob lived for many a year," she wrote. When relating the incident, her dad smiled as he said, "I guess we did a good job."

(right) By the 1960s—120 years after the City of Marion was platted—City Square Park is shrouded by trees. View is from southeast to northwest, same as the bird's eye rendition above.

FOOD FOR THE MIND AND SOUL

Nineteenth century pioneers gave schools and churches top priority. Marion's first school was organized in 1841; first church in 1840. Could a public library be far behind? It was not until sixty years later, in the early 1900s, that a temporary Free Public Library was opened on the second floor in the downtown Owen Block. Early in 1905, the library moved into its own beautiful, new building several blocks east. The railroad came and left Linn County's premier city and an election spirited away its courthouse, but the citizens of Marion—like the pioneer settlers before them—were equal to the challenges.

In the early 1900s, Central Market dominated the corner site on 7th Ave., north of the Square. A variety of businesses, including groceries, barber, insurance, clothing, a funeral parlor and a cafe followed. Second story sign at right identifies Marion's first public library (third window from right).

Schools

The first school was organized in the fall of 1841 in a log building near 14th Street on the north side of what is now Seventh Avenue. In 1854, a four-room brick school building was erected at Fourth Avenue and Eighth Street. Initially called "Union," it was renamed Prescott School. In 1860, Marion was designated an independent school district. By 1900, two types of educational systems served the state and county. Graded elementary and high schools prevailed in towns and villages while ungraded one-room schoolhouses served the rural population. Rural school buildings, distributed around Linn county, were overseen by a County School Superintendent: Lulu B. Secrist retired after serving from 1917 to 1936 and Walter A. Shupp succeeded her. In 1948, seventeen rural schools merged to form what became the Linn-Mar School District. By 2000, Linn-Mar's seven buildings were serving nearly 4,600 students, some of them from Marion. Its 545 employees made Linn-Mar Marion's largest employer. By 2000, Marion Independent had more than 2,000 students and 274 employees including 163 certified teachers. The school systems have become Marion's largest employer.

A 1900s postcard featured Marion's early schools (left to right): Emerson (1891), Lincoln (1868); (bottom) Prescott (1862) and Irving (late 1880s). Prescott served all grades until Lincoln assumed responsibility for upper grades.

In the early 1910s, the boys and girls at Emerson School are photographed. The school was built 20 years earlier on the Richard Thomas Tract to serve the northeast section of the city.

Churches

Marion's Methodist Episcopal Church was organized in 1840, Congregational-Presbyterian 1842 (split later), Baptist 1843, Christian 1844; the Seventh Day Adventist, Congregational and First Presbyterian, all organized in the 1850s. Catholic membership grew when railroad jobs brought many Irish families to Marion. Catholic leaders constructed their first building in 1869 at the southeast corner of Third Avenue and 8th Street. At the beginning of the 21st century, more than two dozen churches of 10 different denominations serve Marion's spiritual needs.

Jobs for Many

The railroad tracks spelled prosperity for those with freight to move and offered the convenience and romance of rail travel for business people and others on the move. The Chicago, Milwaukee, St. Paul and Pacific railroad became a dominant factor that thrived until 1970, having influenced priorities for more than a hundred years. As shipment by road and air gained precedence, many towns and cities— including Marion—and the railroad owners had to adjust to the new situation.

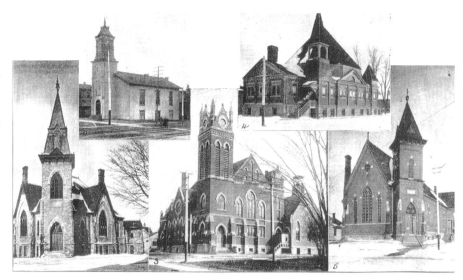

A 1909 picture postcard shows five Marion churches as follows with year built: (from left, top) Baptist (1855), Christian 1896; (bottom) Presbyterian 1884, First Methodist 1895 and Congregational 1877. The Methodists sold their first building (top, left) to the Baptists in 1873; Baptists used it for 85 years.

Postcard mailed in 1916 shows Pacific Limited passenger train arriving. After demolition, the depot roof and bricks were used for constructing the pavilion in City Square Park in 1988.

In the 20th century, old 1714 provided work for the engineer and numerous workmen who proudly drape themselves atop and around their engine.

The Library

The Carnegie Public Library, one of 101 Carnegie-sponsored libraries in Iowa, was the first building dedicated in 1905 to that purpose. Marion's women finally succeeded in realizing their dream after a decade of hard work.

Carnegie Library on 7th Ave. (above) was replaced in 1996 by the new Marion Public Library on 6th Ave. (left, shown with staff and volunteers in front). The Carnegie building served as Marion's library for ninety-one years and is now owned by the Methodist Church. The Library, like the schools and churches, continues to change and meet new challenges.

Around City Square

A devastating fire in 1894 destroyed the eastern three-fourths of the block, opposite City Square Park. Replacement buildings included Iowa's first national bank at the corner of 7th Ave. and 11th. To left of bank, six new storefronts served a variety of businesses in the 20th century. The bank itself moved west on Seventh Ave. and is now a Wells Fargo bank.

Eleventh St., east of the park, changed several times over the years. Now the site of Marion Square Plaza, we see it above as it looked in the 1870s and below before all of the buildings were razed (including the depot extreme right) to make way for new businesses on the Plaza.

City Square Park is decorated for Memorial Day in the 1940s.

DICKEY FAMILY REMEMBERED:

Jean Strong remembers that at least one Mom and Pop grocery remained open Saturday nights in the 1920s and 30s to sack purchases for farm women who socialized with friends until 10 p.m. before selecting next week's needs. Older country children walked with friends around and around the City Square on shopping night, eating treats (popcorn or ice cream lollipops) when money was available, while their mothers visited and their fathers shot some pool at the 11th Street billiard parlor. It was a night to anticipate, a reward for another week of hard work. The entire Dickey family greeted us and obligingly charged our purchases week after week until cash flow from the sale of livestock or grain enabled us to pay the eighty dollar bill that accumulated over a three-month period. L.O. Dickey had purchased the grocery in 1926; he carried my sister and me around the store and always gave us a stick of candy. Other Dickey family members were Mrs. Dickey, son 'Bud,' daughter Francie and her husband Harry B. Jones (later owned Jones Plumbing). After WW II service, Bud Dickey had a grocery in Central City; he later established a dry cleaning business in his family's Marion store. In an interview with Molly Andersen in 2001, Bud said his father came to Marion from southern Iowa to install switching for the railroad. Mom and Pop grocery stores disappeared before Marion's railroad did.

Tenth Street west of the park was altered by fire in 1872. We have a 1920s view (top) of the rebuilt block with the Masonic Temple at center. The 1950s photo (below) shows the Masonic building with its face lift and store fronts. A funeral home is at left and the popular Hallwood Cafe at right.

On 7th Ave., Cira's grocery (four shops east of 10th St.) prevailed for 58 years—from 1909 to 1967. Mike Cira (center) and two sons, Joe (left) and Michael, Jr., present happy faces to customers.

CITY SERVICES EVOLVE

ENHANCING QUALITY OF LIFE

Marion has an enviable record for health and safety over the last century. In 1901, with a population of 5,000, Marion was recognized as the healthiest city in the US. A news release from a federal government agency prompted a Chicago newspaper to send an investigating reporter to ponder 'why?' Marion's death rate of 1.4 per thousand bested nearly twelve hundred other U.S. cities and towns in the 1,000-and-up category. The others averaged a death rate of 17.47 per thousand.

As to 'why,' the reporter concluded that the pure spring water piped in from rural springs west of the city was a true "fountain of youth" and that the mid-city location of the railroad—just a block off the main street—lessened stress for passengers because they did not have far to run for a train. He cited the longevity of several citizens including Richard Thomas who lived well beyond 100 years.

George Owen from New England, a businessman who sponsored a hose company, was a distant relative of the Carl Owen family. He also served as mayor.

FIREFIGHTERS

Marion firefighters have a colorful history. In the 1870s, members of competitive volunteer fire brigades fought fires and competed as drill teams at out-of-town events. Equipment for the volunteer firefighters included hand-drawn carts with a reel of hoses and a hook and ladder.

Better showmen than firefighters, Marion's own Mentzer Drill Team gained national recognition. Dressed in fancy uniforms, the men and their maneuvers were a sight to see. Other teams also bore the names of their sponsors: Phoenix Engine Company, Samuel Saylor Company, B.F. Mentzer Company, J.C. Davis Hook and Ladder Company, George B. Owen Hose Company and Fullerton Hose Company. The city paid $125 to each firefighting company to attend the state tournament and one dollar to the team that first succeeded in getting water running through its hoses at a fire site. Sometimes competitive behavior

The Mentzer Hose Co. in 1895 photo is legendary for its drill team with spiffy costumes. Company memorabilia was lost in the fire of 1922.

The Fullerton Hose Co., wearing drill uniforms, pose with equipment.

resulted in fights over who would get to hook up to the water supply first. Before Marion organized a department in 1876, fires had caused havoc several times in the downtown business area. Fire continued to vex, but the city did not assume responsibility for administrative duties until 1921.

The devastating fire of 1872 destroyed several buildings on 10th Street between Sixth and Seventh avenues; they were replaced by 1880. On 16 September 1881, fire broke out in the Jaquith Opera House on 10th Street, also across from the park, that resulted in $15,000 damage to two tenants (Kinley's billiard hall and Oakley's meat market). Only one third of the losses was insured; the site remained vacant until 1895 when the Masonic Temple was built.

The most disastrous fire in August 1894 occurred when the gas plant blew up, destroying the eastern three-fourths of the Seventh Avenue block opposite City Square and the buildings north on 11th Street to Eighth Avenue. Ironically, among the destroyed buildings were four two-story brick buildings constructed ten years earlier. It was believed that their common walls and tin roofs rendered them fireproof. Only the Owen Building survived. In October 1914, a fire near the Carnegie Library resulted in some damage to the library and the C.A. Pyle Lumber Co. was destroyed. In December 1922, the city-administered fire department was not successful in controlling a fire (called the city's second most destructive) that damaged a grocery and a clothing store. At fault were frozen fire hydrants that produced no water when

In the 21st century, Marion's firefighters number some 50 men and women. Maureen Brown Boots was the first female firefighter to join the department in 1990. Two fire stations are maintained; one on the east side (since 1991), the other on the west side (since the mid 60s). Chief Terry Jackson heads the department (since 1999).

The previous owners of the Sorg Pharmacy: Nathan Sorg, purchased it in 1945 from Carl Owen Estate, sold it to Lois Emanuel in 1975 who sold to Ed and Harriet Morris in 1984.

In 1914, heat and flying embers from the C.A. Pyle Lumber Co. (below) damaged the nine-year-old Carnegie Library. Top photo shows lumber company before fire. Note unpaved 7th Avenue.

41

firemen connected their hoses near the corner of Seventh Avenue and 12th Street.

More recently, in early February 2002, the Park Place antique mall (Balster Building, formerly Daniels Hotel) was severely damaged and a historic pharmacy was also damaged by the fire that began in the early morning hours. The antique mall reopened within a few months of the fire. For a year, while repairs were made, Ed and Harriet Morris, both registered pharmacists, operated their century old pharmacy business from a store-front across the street (in Marion Square Plaza). They also used their Cedar Rapids pharmacy to serve Marion patrons.

Marion's first firehouse in 1876 at current site of Marion Square Plaza shows volunteers on and around the building with two pieces of 'modern' firefighting equipment: a chemical fire engine and a hook and ladder truck, both hand-drawn. Horses weren't readily affordable. The building was purchased from the Baptist Church when the Baptists moved into the vacated Methodist Church building at 6th Ave. and 10th St. (now the Heritage Center).

First big fire of the 21st century took place in the early morning hours of February 2002 damaging the antique mall and a pharmacy. Water is being poured into both buildings from 7th Avenue in this photo.

POLICE DEPARTMENT

Marion also has a record as the 'safest' city in its population class. In earlier days, the town marshal maintained law and order. Marion's Police Department was organized in 1936 with Gene Miller as first chief. By 1940, the department boasted one patrol car for three officers who each worked eight-hour shifts. The department also had a motorcycle with a side-car that Voanne Miller Hansen remembers made a fun ride for a child. This small force did an excellent job. In 1941, Marion was judged the safest city in Iowa in its population class (4,700). Early in World War Two, Chief Miller resigned. Wartime demands had claimed all suitable candidates and Mayor John Mullin assisted with police

Police Chief Harry Daugherty attributes the declining crime rate over the past several years to community policing and public support, the work ethic of members of the department and support with equipment and staffing from the City Council.

In 2004 the department boasts twenty-two vehicles and forty-seven employees including 38 sworn officers and a nine-member support staff.

Marion Police Department patrol car in 1940.

work for the duration. In 1999, Marion had the lowest crime rate in Iowa among cities with over-20,000 population (FBI Uniform Crime Report). In 2003, Marion again was named safest city among thirty-three with 20,000-plus population. With crime so low (18 per thousand) it's little surprise that 98 percent of Marion citizens say, in the 2004 survey conducted by the city manager, "Marion is a nice place to live." And nearly 93 percent of those surveyed want Marion to maintain its own identity as it has consciously done for the past 20 years or more.

Waterworks tower under construction in 1886 shows four men atop the standpipe before the storage tank was added. Triangle at right seems to be a lift that took the men to the top.

Water Department

Wells were the source of Marion's water supply until 1886 when spring water began to be pumped in from the rural countryside. In 1952, Marion returned to wells as its water source. In 2004, more than 50 years later, six deep wells and four pumping stations do the job. The system has four ground storage tanks with a total capacity of 2.2-million gallons and three elevated storage tanks with 2-million gallons capacity. An average of 2.3-million gallons is pumped daily for 10,000 metered accounts through a 135-mile network of water mains and 1,095 fire hydrants. The department has a director and is governed by a three-member citizens' Board of Trustees, appointed by the mayor, approved by the council. Administrative offices are located in City Hall.

George and Alyce Lowe donated their farm land between North 10th Street and Alburnett Road for a new Marion Community Park.

Parks Department

The Parks Department manages 18 city parks, Oak Shade Cemetery, the Community Center, Willowood Pool and the

Boyson hiking-biking trail. The Community Center, formerly Washington Irving grade school, houses the parks department's administrative offices. A new multi-use park is in the works thanks to the generosity in 2001 of George and Alyce Lowe who donated 182 acres of farmland north of Marion to be developed as a community park. The following year, daughter Katie Lowe-Lancaster, Mayor Klopfenstein and City Councilman John Nieland were among many community leaders who raised thousands of dollars in donations from private citizens to help get Lowe Park through initial planning stages. The development plan includes four phases over 20 years.

Post Office

Marion's Post Office relocated many times during its 165 years of existence, from the first at the Strong Inn on Central Avenue and the second at Daniel's downtown general store on 10th Street to the current (since December 2001) post office in east Marion. Mary Mentzer Hollingsworth (1875-1943) was the first woman 'postmaster' from 1937 to 1943. Born into the prominent Ben Mentzer family and a niece of Adeliza Daniels, she was of independent mind and known for voicing her opinions. She and her husband, Elmer Hollingsworth, operated the Boston Store on Seventh Avenue between 11th and 12th streets. When Mrs. Hollingsworth suffered a heart attack, newspaperwoman Grace Koppenhaver was appointed to serve out her term.

Marion's **fund-raising** efforts for park facilities in 2002 also secured a $750,000 award from Vision Iowa for the Arts and Environment Center that will be the main component of Lowe Community Park, encompassing 11acres of the 182-acre park site.

Vision Iowa is a state program of the Iowa Economic Development Department providing financial incentives to communities for construction of facilities that enhance the quality of life.

Mary Mentzer Hollingsworth, Marion's first postmistress, was a graduate of Cornell College. She was first regent for Marion-Linn Chapter D.A.R. and a member of the Ameigo and Therestriai clubs as well as the Chapter CS, P.E.O. She died in office in 1943.

This was the first building dedicated (1938) as a Post Office. Since the 1970s, the building has been Marion's City Hall. A new city hall is planned.

BEYOND CITY SQUARE

In the beginning, the county courthouse and a city square dominated town center. Even as business developed in and around Marion, some expansion occurred westward toward Cedar Rapids. After the Civil War, Isaac Kramer chose to settle west of Indian Creek on the north side of Marion Boulevard. This enterprising pioneer built the first greenhouse in Linn County in 1863 on his 40-acre homestead, five miles northwest of Marion, seven miles north of Cedar Rapids. He enjoyed a good business from residents of both towns who "probably came for an outing as well as to get plants," he surmised.

A big hail storm in 1867 broke up the greenhouses he constructed with 'imperfect' panes of broken glass purchased from Addison Daniels. The loss caused Isaac to change locations before he was financially ready. Preferring to locate in Cedar Rapids, he could not bring himself to commit to the site he favored. So he chose Marion because the five acres were "available with no down payment," he wrote. "The site was covered with stumps, and there was no house on it. I had no money to build one, and a family to support. The lumber man and merchants of Marion, by generous credit, helped me through. By gardening among the stumps as best I could, I sold vegetable and sweet potato plants, and was able to meet all of my contracts and pay some on my land." By the early 1900s, Isaac had replaced his first modest home with a grand Victorian one.

Other business men also chose sites west of Thomas Park: Kemble's, then Bezdek's in the late 1930s were successors to Isaac N. Kramer & Son. The George Kaiser Wayside Gardens was on

Kemble's purchased the Kramer operation after Isaac's only son succumbed to a heart attack, while delivering flowers in Marion, in 1920. Judson had been cranking his delivery truck.

the south side at top of the hill across from the site of Todd's OK Drive-In and Herb's Barbecue. Armar Ballroom and an amusement park were also located west of Thomas park.

Henry Katz and his brother, Bert, led the expansion eastward from downtown as they established in the 1940s a salvage business and an attractive mobile home park along Highway 151 east. The first supermarket (Sun Mart) followed in the 1950s. In the 21st century, business expansion continues eastward and north into the once rural countryside along Highway 13.

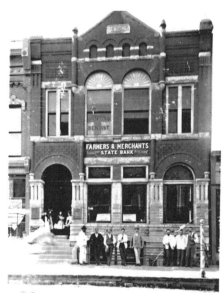

In 1894, after the Daniels Bank failed, the Farmers & Merchants State Bank (above) was organized at 1135 7th Ave; it ceased operating in the 1930s. Farmers State Bank began operating in this building in 1945 after 18 years as a state bank in Alburnett. In 1966, Farmers State Bank moved to its new building at 8th Ave and 12th St. (Only Marion's First National Bank survived the 1930s depression).

Maier's Farm Implement store on south side of Seventh Ave. between 12th and 13th streets displays a buggy and push lawn mower.

In 1915, looking east toward Marion. Beyond the sturdy new bridge over Indian Creek we see an unpaved Sixth Ave. Marion was still the county seat but Cedar Rapids had grown larger and in four more years would win the election that gave them the courthouse.

IN TOWN CENTER many old businesses have been replaced, but downtown Marion continues as a vibrant part of Marion today. Within one or two blocks of City Square, you can borrow books or use a computer at the public library, visit the Heritage Center, get a blood test or a haircut, shop for antique treasures, browse used book stores, buy fresh flowers or choose a painting or piece of art at the gallery. If you need a break, you can also get something good to eat and drink.

Picture postcard of Seventh Avenue in the 1920s shows 'Boulevard' street lights, a fire hydrant and Ed Sigfred's storefront at left.

The 1920s dining room of the C.C. Miller Cafe, on Sixth Ave. and 12th St., was probably where Carrie Davis Reichert and her mother, Mrs. J.C. Davis, "ate chicken dinner every Sunday" after their spouses died.

In 1890s Marion, rigs for hire were a common sight. This team and carriage on 8th Ave. near 9th St. is from the Groll and Oxley Livery.

This cigar salesman was passing through town in one of the first cars seen on Marion streets. In the background is the historic Owen Drug Store that became Sorg Pharmacy in 1945. It moved one store west in 1954.

Impact on Society

An Enduring Love Affair

America's love affair with the automobile began in the early 1900s and continues in the 21st century as air pollution, gasoline shortages and overcrowded roadways pose challenges for everyone. Dozens of car makers competed for buyers, but it was Henry Ford's Model-T that first brought cars within reach of the average buyer, selling for $290 and up. Linn County buyers exhibited discerning choices and black was the only color.

In 1910, proud owners and friends line 7th Ave. displaying their cars. By 1918, 50 different companies had manufactured the 750 autos registered in Linn County.

Like It Was in the 1920s

A young Marion farm lad named Walter Strong was in his teens when he acquired his first automobile, a 1916 two-seater Ford roadster with hard rubber tires. At age 19 he met his future wife in the George Kaiser shoe store in Cedar Rapids. Kaiser's wife (Lettie) was a sister of Walter Strong's stepmother. On this Saturday night, Walter came to the store basement to buy overshoes. Thelma Oliver, George Kaiser's bookkeeper (from 1917 to 1921), went downstairs on an errand and Abbie Kaiser, who had a shoe repair business there, introduced them and suggested

C.W. Court & Son Livery on 11th St. near Eighth Ave. is the backdrop for this confrontation of the 'horseless' and horse-drawn carriage. Court's livery was one of several stables around the city at the turn of the century. The remodeled building remains as a storefront for several businesses including Marion's Chamber of Commerce.

The Marion Garage was one of the earliest for the Automobile Age.

St. Berchmans Boarding School at 1501 First Ave. numbered among its students two boys who became Hollywood movie stars. Don Ameche and Don DeFore attended at different times. In the 1920s photo below, boys and a chaplain await the train that will take them to Chicago for the holidays. Neither passenger nor freight train service endured for Marion in the 21st century and St. Berchmans became an apartment house.

he take her out. The pair agreed to meet the next day at the Kaiser home on Sixth Ave., Marion. Thelma and a girl friend, Viola Smith (Matteson), had planned a three-mile Sunday walk from their northeast side homes to Thomas Park; the Kaiser home was only a few blocks farther east. Two years later (6 October 1921), Walter and Thelma eloped to Vinton in neighboring Benton County; the roadster broke down on the way back to Cedar Rapids. A passing glassware salesman guessed that they were newlyweds and took them to the home of Thelma's sister and brother-in-law where she had a room. Although Walter's parents had entertained the bride numerous times at Sunday supper during their courtship (while Walter did his Sunday chores), the young man kept their secret for several months. When his father learned of the union, he altered his plan to convert the old Bowman-Strong homestead into a corn crib and, instead, created a two-room home with an unfinished upstairs. The couple moved into the little house on the farm one mile northwest of Marion in 1922. Their five children were born in the same house as Walter and his brother.

The Power of Perseverance—and Women

A Marion Federation of Women's Clubs, formed in 1901 to obtain a library, dedicated its efforts to other city projects as well (park and cemetery). The ladies' proudest moment came in 1917 when they purchased the lot west of the library by outwitting a businessman who wanted it. The Federation persisted for more than 50 years before it was disbanded. Among the 10 or so member groups was the oldest ladies' study club in Iowa, organized in 1867 as the Young Ladies Literary Society. It became the O.O.P. and with the Therestriai was among the original coalition of clubs. The O.O.P. still actively supports the library.

Miss Alexander

Mabel Alexander, O.O.P. member and Marion's second librarian, immortalized places and people in her 1940 book about *My Town*. Among them: Pegleg Rose, Lizzie Marshall and the Cherry Sisters. She was living elsewhere, but Marion and its people were dear to her heart.

Unforgettable Characters

Richard Thomas, 1782-1892

Born in Baltimore County, Maryland, Richard Thomas immigrated to Iowa Territory in 1837, settled in Marion in the 1840s at age 58 and died there at age 110 after a remarkable life. In 1814, he witnessed the burning of Washington, DC and nearly lost an arm in an accident with the waterwheel while building Marion's first sawmill on Indian Creek in 1841. He married in 1865 at age 83 a woman 50 years younger than he was (Julia Jones). She died in 1926. Their daughter, Mary Thomas, married a doctor, Bell English, and gave 'Uncle Dickie' two grandsons. Mary lived to be 97; she died some years after her husband and two sons.

Sylvester P. "Lev" Leverich, 1853-1940

[Excerpted from Marvin Oxley's *Marion History, Vol. 3, 1880-1889*]

To the 1930's generation, S.P. Leverich was a near-blind, poverty-threatened old man, deserted by his family. More observant old timers saw an undaunted spirit with a still useful brain housed in a shabby but pretentious body. Marion never seriously disapproved of him because one's wits had to be sharper with such a person around. [During his active years Lev was in real estate and served on the City Council.] Stories of Lev's escapades became part of the town saga.

An urchin stopped to stare. Lev returned the interest and inquired, "Boy, how old are you?" When the lad replied, Lev said, "I don't believe it; no one could get that dirty in seven years." Another day his legs gave out near the livery barn. With a ten-dollar bill, Lev induced Charlie Dumont, the undertaker's son, to load him into the hearse, and drive him about town. He said he wanted to know how it felt to be dead.

Lev usually disliked personal publicity but, if he could see well enough to discover people watching him, he would take the street car to Cedar Rapids, and work out his schemes there. It is said he stood on a prominent street corner for nearly an hour offering to sell a ten dollar bill for a five. On another alcoholic occasion, Lev stood gazing down upon the industrious shoemaker, Kaiser. Lev remembered that he had promised two weeks ago to "throw something his way" in return for some trifling free repair work.

Richard Thomas at 102 with 2-year-old grandson in 1884. 'Uncle Dickie' lived another eight years—a hardy pioneer personified. Thomas Park is named for him.

Voanne Hansen Remembers—As a youngster Voanne remembers their neighbor, Mary English: "She always had a Boston Terrier named Beans—several dogs but the name remained the same."

Poems by Mabel Alexander, 1940

Miss Marshall

Her real name was Elizabeth,
But she signed herself "Lizzie R."
She was Dr. Marshall's daughter
And her influence went so far
That she touched, I think, without
　　a doubt,
More people in My Town and
　　round about,
Than any other person…
…And lived in every way
A paragon of character,
And a person destined to stay
In the minds of those who knew
　　her,
Until their dying day.

In 1918, Lev Leverich (left) poses with his family in front of their home on the southeast corner of 6th Ave. at 7th St.: Daughter Marnie P. Dunbar, wife Mary K. Leverich, daughters Edna (McGill Simpson Winz), Grace Bixby, and Pauline Barros, and son-in-law Allen David Barros. Mr. Leverich died in 1940.

Lev grasped a large cobblestone and tossed it through the window of Kaiser's basement shop, narrowly missing his foot. He thought some boys had tried to kill him. Lev tried in vain to explain his promise to the old German—and then had a new $4.00 sash installed.

THE CHERRY SISTERS (1893 to 1908 Heyday)

Marion's Cherry Sisters are arguably the most unforgettable among the unforgettable. The sisters evoked passions ranging from pity to ridicule as they kept Marion on the national 'entertainment' map for about 15 years. Carrie Davis (Reichert) witnessed their maiden performance in Marion's Daniels Opera House on Seventh Avenue with her father. "The house was packed and the people made more noise than they do at a ballgame today," she wrote. "They threw vegetables at them. A piece of raw liver hit Effie in the stomach as she clung to the cross and she said: 'I don't care; we have your money.'" News reports said they netted $100 from that dramatic performance.

From this beginning, the sisters' act went on the road to Greene's Opera House in Cedar Rapids and to New York City where their manager (manager of Cedar Rapids Country Club) booked them at the famous Hammerstein Opera House. In

ELLEN, THE STAY-AT-HOME CHERRY

All the years the Sisters were
     touring
Ellen kept the home fires bright,
And she often came to "My Town"
On business, day and night.
She and my father were very
     good friends,
"Ellen's banker," we sometimes
     called him.
She'd borrow on Monday, on
     Friday repay...

The next time Mabel saw Ellen
"on an Autumn day," she wrote:

...leading a cow, she passed our
     door
On the way to their farm,
Three miles or more.
And one day in a street car,
Across the aisle from me,
A live chicken in a basket
Ellen held upon her knee.
She was trying to read a letter,
The chicken trying to get out,
I was highly entertained
Watching their little bout.
I smiled at Ellen, she smiled at
     me,
For she too enjoyed the comedy.

THE PERFORMING CHERRY SISTERS

They spoke with an Eastern accent,
and tho they had an air all their
     own,
They were probably surprised
     themselves
When they brought "My Town"
     renown—

(continued top of next page)

Queens of Comedy and Song,
THE RENOWNED

Cherry Sisters.

The Company are ole authors of the entire Program.

PROGRAMME

ACT I.
Tableau..................................Clinging to the Cross

ACT II.
Solo—Chicago, Composed and Sung by......Effie Cherry
Solo—Bicycle ride to the Fair, composed and
    Sung by.................................Jessie Cherry

ACT III.
Tableau—Autumn Scene....................Ella Cherry

ACT IV.
Recitation—Corn Juice, composed by.......Jessie Cherry
Essay—Modern Young Man by....Addie and Effie Cherry
Solo—Fair Columbia, composed and sung by Jessie Cherry
Old Woman's Opinion,...........Addie and Effie Cherry
Music......................................Jessie Cherry

ACT V.
Irish Ballad by Lizzie Cherry, sung by Addie
    ....and Effie Cherry
Irish Lassie by Lizzie Cherry, sung by......Jessie Cherry
Hunting Scene..............Addie and Jessie Cherry
Solo—When I Asked her if I Might, composed
    and sung by............................Effie Cherry
The Editor.................Addie and Jessie Cherry
    Dedicated to Fred Faulkes, editor of the "Evening
    Gazette," Cedar Rapids, Iowa.

ACT VI.
Solo—The Railroad Boys, composed and sung
    ....by Effie Cherry
Solo—Bonnie Lassie, composed and sung by Jessie Cherry
Solo—The Traveling Man, composed by....Effie Cherry
Barefooted Iona, the Orphan Flower Girl....Jessie Cherry
Eulogy on the Cherry Sisters, composed by
    Lizzie Cherry, sung by......Addie and Effie Cherry

ACT VII.
Two Grand Tableaux.
    National—The Goddess of Liberty and Her Subjects,
        by Lizzie, Effie and Jessie Cherry.
    Sacred—Faith, Hope and Charity.

ENDORSED BY PULPIT AND PRESS. LADIES
    ESPECIALLY INVITED.

Effie Cherry in 1896, a star performer with her three sisters. The programme lists the seven acts in their unchanging repertoire.

their New York performance, "Addie and Lizzie appeared in blue print gowns to sing what was billed as an Irish ballad." Despite audience howls of simulated agony, "the girls bravely stuck to their work, seemingly undisturbed by the chaos, and not a trace of laughter or anger was shown in their faces…to emphasize their independence each sang in a different key, both totally unmindful of the orchestra."

A *New York Times* movie reviewer might have been describing their performances when he wrote about a movie titled "A Mighty Wind" in 2003. The players, he wrote "are immune to embarrassment and utterly devoted to their own peculiar notions of artistic accomplishment and show-business glory. They are, it must be said, pretty good at making bad music."

The Sisters made lots of money,
Tho their managers took it all,
But they kept on undaunted
Starting their tours in the Fall.
They never changed their
    repertoire,
The same crude stunts they gave,
And every year their rating fell
But they were always brave.

… Sometimes they showed at
    County Fairs,
But at last, their youth long gone,
They were compelled to quit "the
    stage"
And face oblivion.

…Now all is changed
Their farm's run down,
Effie was next to die,
And efficient Ellen, not long ago,
Her pride hurt, sad to say,
Breathed her last at the County
    Home.
But their house dilapidated,
Was no place for a person ill,
And the doctor, to insure good
    care,
Moved her there to the hospital.
The two Sisters left, forlornly,
Sometimes walk a Marion street,
Queer old-fashioned figures,
With not many friends to greet,
For "My Town" has changed
And the people too.

…So Fate turns her wheel of
    fortune.
It goes both up and down,
These Sisters who enjoyed her
    smile
Now live to see Her Frown.

—excerpts from poems by
Mabel Alexander, 1940

Patriots and Parades

Ten wars have been fought since Marion was founded: Mexican, Civil, Spanish American, World War One, World War Two, Korean, Vietnam, Gulf I, Afghanistan and Gulf II (Iraq again). Linn county citizens have participated in most, if not all. In addition to General McKean's leadership in the Civil War, Hosea W. Gray, 45, in April 1861 organized the Marion Light Guard that was sworn into service in July with Gray as captain. In 1862 at the Battle of Shiloh in Tennessee, three of Gray's men were killed, 13 wounded and three taken prisoner. A Civil War monument in City Square Park overlooks the avenue of parades that is main street. One cannon still graces the west side of the park; a second cannon and cannon balls were relinquished for scrap during WW II. Since 1989, an annual parade celebrates Marion's past; it is one event during the three-day Swamp Fox Festival.

Lieutenant Colonel Bill Reed (1917-1944)

William Norman Reed was honored at "Bill Reed Day" in Marion on 19 September 1942 after serving for six and one-half months as one of Claire Chenault's Flying Tigers. Reed had resigned his air force commission in 1941 to be one of the American Volunteer Group that was fighting against the Japanese two weeks after the Pearl Harbor attack. According to one of several Flying Tiger web sites, Reed and 67 other members of the famous flying group received bonuses for their work. Reed is credited with destroying 10.5 enemy planes and making three air-to-air kills.

Reed arrived late for the parade, but he and his mother were honored guests at a banquet held at the Indian Creek Country Club. After hearing the flyer speak, one guest said, "That boy has sure seen a lot and he knows how to tell about it." Following his day in Marion, Reed set off on a War Bonds tour. He reentered the U.S. Army Air Force in 1943 with the rank of major. Shot down that same year, he spent three weeks returning to base. After visiting Marion in July 1943, he returned to duty and was promoted to lieutenant colonel.

Born 8 January 1917 in Stone City, Reed graduated from Marion High School in 1935 and in 1939 from Columbia College (now Loras). He first entered the air force in 1940. After the war, Reed had hoped to pursue a business career in China, but that was not

Since 1914, the Soldiers' and Sailors' monument has overlooked Seventh Avenue—the avenue of parades—from City Square Park.

This Civil War memorial was erected under the auspices of the Robert Mitchell Post No. 206 and of Robert Mitchell, W.R. Corps No. 126, the Grand Army of the Republic (GAR).

to be. On 19 December 1944, thirty days shy of his 28th birthday, Bill Reed was lost "somewhere in China."

Flyer Bill Reed's parade (left) and the flyer (above).

Veterans lead a parade between 12th and 11th streets as spectators line 7th Avenue.

Three of the four WW I veterans, marching abreast as the color guard in this 1920 Memorial Day parade, became leaders in Marion. From left are Celan Rollins, John Pazour (future mayor and postmaster), A.R. McElwain (elected American Legion commander in 1919), and Gene Miller who became Marion's first chief of police 16 years later. This was Marion's first Memorial Day parade after American Legion Post 298 received its charter in 1919.

LEISURE PURSUITS

A sampling of entertainment opportunities in Marion over the decades show that life was good because people cared—and still do. Musical events have been consistently popular through the years: chamber groups, band concerts in the park and dancing to the nation's big bands. City Square Park's first band concert took place in 1886 and two groups—Marion Big Band and Marion Community Band—continue with musicians of all ages. Shows in front of a grandstand delighted thousands of racing fans and fair goers for nearly a quarter century at Marion's Interstate Fair Grounds. The "eating-out" experience of the 20s and 30s became less formal as busy people demanded food on the fly. Picnics in area parks have not gone out of fashion but the attire of picnickers has changed. Marion's biggest downtown show ever—the Marion Corn Festival of the 1940s—remained unrivaled as a successful three-day attraction until townspeople in 1989 launched the Swamp Fox Festival. Held each September, the new event brings a festive air to the entire city.

Moving pictures first lured fun-seeking Marionites from their homes into movie theaters during World War One. Television in the 50s tended to entice people back into their homes. Through the years since 1905, Marion's free public library has provided reading entertainment opportunities. Additional media and services, made possible by new technologies, attract ever-increasing numbers of patrons. In the 21st century, the facility is poised for growth to meet community demands.

FAIR ASSOCIATION

In October 1900, prominent businessmen formed the Marion Interstate Fair Association to organize fairs and carnivals. Until then, the old fair grounds, east of town, had served since the 1870s. Enthused citizens contributed $10,000 for improving the fair grounds. The Association paid Earl Granger $6,725 for 11 acres of land north of Marion and, in spring 1901, built a half-mile race track and a 192-foot-long grandstand to seat 2400 patrons. Marion's first Interstate Fair took place in September of that year. Cattle and horse barns, an agricultural hall and secretary's office building were added. The new fairgrounds accommodated numerous events including high school athletic contests for nearly a quarter century. Indian Creek Country Club opened on the site in 1925.

Chamber music by the Apollo Mandolin Club flourished for five years from 1898 to 1903 with a youthful Marvin Oxley (far right) as one of the musicians. Other players from left: James Welsh, Harold Oxley, Herbert Carver and Leonard Carr.

In 1907, overflow crowds fill the spacious grandstand seating 2400 patrons at Marion's Interstate Fair Grounds. Horse racing was a popular event. Judging stand at right provided a good view of the half-mile race track.

Colorful Iowa corn adorned the bandstand in City Square Park for the ambitious three-day Corn Festival programs of the 1940s. This "Corn Palace" helped advertise the event.

The Garden Theatre in 1980s, on 10th St. between 7th and 8th avenues, had operated for more than 60 years since WW I days.

Corn Festivals in 1940s

In 1940, the executive secretary of Marion's Chamber of Commerce organized the first Marion Corn Festival. Held in and around City Square Park, it lasted three days. Marion's biggest-ever celebration, featuring extensive free acts and carnival rides, attracted thousands from Eastern Iowa. John C. Mullin (1889-1970), the Chamber executive who originated the first of these popular fall celebrations, was elected wartime mayor in 1941 and served until he resigned in 1947; he became manager of Marion's first liquor store. Corn Festivals were held again in 1941, 1948 and 1949. In 1951, a one-day event ended the corn festival era. A Council Bluffs native, Mullin had been employed by the Chicago, Milwaukee and St. Paul Railroad, served as a district manager for Anheuser-Busch Company and was a WW I army veteran.

Theatre 'Bank Nites'

During the Depression Years of the 1930s and 40s, patrons paid a few cents for a double feature movie and a chance to win dollars on 'Bank Nites' at Marion's Garden Theatre. Drawings picked lucky winners for cash prizes.

Cemar Acres on the Boulevard featured children's rides from 1952 to 1968.

SWIMMING HOLE

Skinny-dipping boys who swam beneath the bridge on Alburnett Road were given an alternative in 1930 when the American Legion built a large pool adjacent to Thomas Park. After 55 years it developed leaks beyond repair, partially caused by flooding in Indian Creek. An indoor pool at the YMCA on 10th Ave. at 31st St. and the east side outdoor Marion Municipal Pool in Willowood Park are popular in the 21st century.

FIELD DAY AT THOMAS PARK

In the late 30s, rural school pupils competed at a field day in Thomas Park. Running, ball throwing, high and broad jumping (both standing and running) were among the events for which blue, red and white ribbons were awarded the top three winners in each event. Jean Strong still has her multicolored ribbon collection. City children have enjoyed Easter egg hunts in the park for many years.

This 1920s picture postcard touts Thomas Park as a "tourist park." It has been a popular recreation site for 84 years.

The A & W Root Beer Drive-in location of the 1950s, at 100 6th Ave., is now occupied by a fast-food McDonald's.

Men about town, c. 1915, probably did not look like these seven high school boys who seem intent on having fun. From left: 1. Celan Rollins, 2. Lumir Schultz, 3. ?, 4. Lyman Smith, 5. and 6. ? and 7. Dayton Lininger are posing on 7th Ave. across from the City Square. Why ARE they dressed this way?

Eastern Iowans danced to the trumpet of Harry James and his Music Makers at the grand opening of the Armar Ballroom in late 1948. Sixty different Big Bands plus local groups like Leo Greco, Johnny Ketelsen and Kenny Hofer entertained at balls for Cedar Rapids and Marion police and firemen, Coe and Cornell college dances and Marion High School prom. Dinners for Linn Cooperative Oil Company and the Marion Chamber of Commerce were also among the special events. Dancing continued here through the early 60s.

ARMAR BALLROOM

In the 1950s, New York City had its notable Roseland ballroom on West 52nd Street and Marion had its Armar on the Boulevard. The magnificent Marion ballroom, built by Des Moines' Tom Archer, featured a 7500 square foot sunken dance floor and terraced table and booth seating for 1600 patrons. Archer obtained framework and truss assemblies for the building through government war surplus from an air force base in South Dakota; they were shipped by rail to Marion and erected on the 11-acre site. People came to Marion from all over Eastern Iowa to dance to music of the big and local bands. A large revolving ball hanging above the dance floor added a romantic glow to indirect peripheral lighting of rose, gold and blue hues. Air conditioning was included in the price of admission, a welcome added attraction on hot summer nights. Even as ballroom dancing declined nationwide in the 50s, Armar enjoyed "big box office" into the 60s as Eastern Iowans danced on to rhythms and melodies they enjoyed.

STREET ENTERTAINMENT

For an eight-year-old girl, the street entertainment on Seventh Ave. in the early 1930s was a wondrous sight. A Ferris wheel and other carnival rides lined the side streets, but the most memorable skill was displayed by the oriental tumbling act on a stage fronting several Marion businesses. Unmindful of how

Roller rink at Cemar Acres Amusement Park was operated by Don and Clista McElhinney for many years. Skaters paid as little as 10 cents to skate on Saturday nights and Sunday afternoons.

Carnegie Library float in early September 1989 Sesquicentennial Parade proclaims: "Reading is not a thing of the past." Sponsors of this winning entry are listed at left. O.O.P. members, seated at right, are reading. Library executive Susan Kling is seated behind boy in white hat (center). In subsequent years, the celebration became an annual event called the Swamp Fox Festival.

the event came about, the girl was awed by the little men who bounced and somersaulted across the stage, sometimes through the air without touching feet to stage. She also remembers walking through the crowd and spotting a five dollar bill on the ground at the feet of a man with child in arms. She picked it up and asked, "Did you drop this?" With nary a "thank you," he pocketed the bill and continued watching the entertainment. In retrospect, the girl thought the man had not dropped the five dollar bill, but he probably needed it more than she did. The Depression was in full swing and her farm family never went hungry although ready cash was usually in short supply for everyone. Farm folk planted large gardens and butchered their own beef and pork.

COMMUNITY PARK IS COMING
More than a dozen Marion parks have been developed since the first in 1921. The newest and largest—Lowe Community Park—is on the drawing boards with a 20-year development plan. The first million of the required $12.9 million has been raised from generous supporters.

MARION HIGHLIGHTS

Marble letters adorned a grassy area to greet train travelers east of the Marion depot in 1910s, before addition was built to depot.

CITY AND COUNTY CENSUS NUMBERS

Census counts for Linn County and the City of Marion over 15 decades illustrate how the city kept pace with the area growth. Marion claimed 13.7 percent of the county population by the year 2000.

Year	Marion	County	%City
1850	n/a	5,444	n/a
1860	1,367	18,947	7.2
1870	1,822	31,080	5.8
1880	1,939	37,237	5.2
1890	3,094	45,303	6.8
1900	4,102	55,392	7.4
1910	4,400	60,720	7.2
1920	4,138	74,004	5.6
1930	4,348	83,336	5.2
1940	4,721	89,142	5.3
1950	5,916	104,274	5.7
1960	10,882	136,899	7.9
1970	18,028	163,213	11.0
1980	19,474	169,775	11.5
1990	20,422	168,767	12.1
2000	26,294	191,701	13.7

1839

- In April, Marion becomes the fourth city organized in Linn County and is sole survivor of the four in the 21st century. Other towns were Westport, Columbus and Ivanhoe.
- Luman M. Strong builds the first home and inn on the south side of Central Avenue on east bank of Indian Creek. William K. Farnsworth, the first settler in Marion, did not build the first house.

1840

- Luman Strong is appointed first postmaster 7 March.
- Addison Daniels builds Marion's second store on 10th street, north of the Dickey building. (William H.) Woodbridge and Thompson had the first store.
- First saw mill in Linn County is established on west bank of Indian Creek by Hiram Beales and Richard "Uncle Dickie" Thomas.
- First courthouse is under construction at Sixth Avenue and 10th street; completed in 1841.

1841

- First school organized in the fall, a log building located north side of what is now Seventh Avenue near 14th St.

1842

- Addison Daniels named second postmaster on 11 May. Post office in his 10th Street store.

1843

- Baptist Church organized in Marion.

1846

- The second courthouse (Greek revival architecture, brick construction) completed on Sixth Avenue; cost $3,152. It was between 10th and 11th streets, east of the first courthouse.
- Iowa becomes the 29th state in the union; county population is 3,411.
- Thomas J. McKean, West Point graduate, is training a squad for the Mexican War.

1847

- The 'Marion meteorite' falls nine miles south of town in Putnam Township (Section 20, Range 6). The first of five meteorites that fell in Iowa, this one broke into several pieces ranging from 2 to 46 pounds.

1850

- Addison Daniels, pioneer merchant, major land owner and speculator, sold a lot for $60 to the Presbyterians for their first church building on 10th street north of Sixth Avenue, opposite City Park.
- Marion is booming "primarily because of its importance as the county seat."

1851

- Methodist Church purchased first courthouse building to use until their church is built.

1852

- First newspaper published in Marion: *The Prairie Star*, Whig paper, Azor Hoyt, owner and publisher. Before year's end J.S. and H.H. Jenison purchased the paper; renamed it *The Linn County Register*.

1853

- Work begins on the railroad tracks and a new boom began in 1854.
- A new rope ferry built by Albert Blair south of Palo provided convenient access for travelers going west.

1854

- The four-room brick "Union" school building is erected on Fourth Avenue and 8th Street.

1855

- First election contest for the county seat occurred. County Judge James Berry of Marion controlled business affairs in the county; he defeated Elias Skinner, Cedar Rapids minister, and Marion prevailed as the court house site.
- First services are held in the new Presbyterian Church on 10th Street.

1856

- The Marion Steam Mill on 11th Street and First Avenue obtained its water supply from a nearby spring-fed creek; it is the only grist mill within three miles.

1858

- Fourth of July celebration is held at Isbell's Grove, south of Marion.

1859

- First train steamed into Cedar Rapids on 15 June, more than five years before train service reached Marion.

1860

- Marion named an independent school district.
- Ice cream is first mentioned in the newspaper regarding an entertainment in Union Hall of the New Hotel.
- Miss Adelaide Isbell opens a private school for advanced scholars whose parents can afford the cost.

1861

- Hosea W. Gray, 45, organized The Marion Light Guards in April; they were sworn into service for the Civil War in July with Gray as captain. In 1862 the unit listed 3 killed, 13 wounded and 3 prisoners at the Battle of Shiloh in Tennessee.
- Land is purchased for a "poor farm" 4 miles northeast of Marion; known as Linn County Home. [Early in the 1900s Gene and Faye Isham became long-time administrator and care-takers at the home.]
- Passenger pigeons in the woods south of Marion are the target for many hunters; the pigeons were said to be excellent eating.

1863

- Marion population (2,870) still exceeds that of Cedar Rapids (1,610). Marion also has more dwellings: 497 to 329.
- First National Bank is founded as Iowa's first enduring national bank. [In 1983, it was sold to Norwest Corp., which in 2000 sold it to Wells Fargo.]

1864

- First train of the Dubuque Southwestern Railway pulls into Marion on 13 October.
- Captain Rathbun purchased the newspaper; changed its name to *The Marion Register*.
- The new Marion Fair Grounds are established on six acres east of town. (S.W. corner of 7th Ave & 31st St. South.)

1865

- Marion incorporated; elects Thomas J. McKean first mayor when the general returned from Civil War service.
- Milwaukee railroad track is laid between Marion and Cedar Rapids.
- William Downing is mentioned in *The Register* as librarian of Marion Library Association (rental library?). Downing is also postmaster with the post

office in his book store (Yearnshaw's). He and his brother, Thomas, had arrived in Marion in 1840 and bought property.

1867

- Isaac N. Kramer, florist and nurseryman, cleared 15 acres west of Indian Creek for gardens, greenhouses and a home.
- Luman M. Strong, Marion pioneer from 1839 to 1848, died in Dodgeville, Wisconsin where he was serving his third term as Iowa County judge.

1868

- Lincoln School building is ready for use.

1869

- Catholics construct their first church at the southeast corner of Third Avenue and 8th Street.

1870

- Marion's first mayor, Brig. General Thomas J. McKean, died at 60.

1872

- A $10,000 fire destroys several 10th Street buildings between Sixth and Seventh avenues; by 1880 they were rebuilt.
- The Milwaukee railroad line extends to Marion. A second passenger depot is constructed between Sixth and Seventh avenues and 18th and 19th streets.

1873

- The Joseph Mentzer family built a store at 10th Street and Seventh Avenue. Over the years it housed a succession of grocery stores and a dry cleaning business when it was known as the Dickey building.

1874

- A well and town pump supplied water for the city from 1874 until 1886.

1876

- Marion's first firehouse is converted Baptist Church on 11th Street. This site is now the southwest corner of the Marion Square Plaza.

1877

- Sixth Avenue west, between Marion and Cedar Rapids, was completed and named The Boulevard.

1879

- Construction began on a street railway along The Boulevard; on 12 April 1880 the first interurban car service, pulled by steam engines and horses, carried passengers between the rival cities.

1881

- Railroad construction causing a boom in Marion.
- Fire erupted in the Jaquith Opera House on 10th street, across from the park, on 16 September 1881. Two tenants, Kinley's billiard hall and Oakley's meat market, sustained $15,000 damage with only $5,500 covered by insurance. [The site remained vacant until 1895 when the Masonic Temple was built.]

1883

- New railroad depot is completed along Sixth Avenue at corner of 11th Street (firehouse site).
- Switch yards and shops are built east of the depot after Marion was designated a 'division point' by the Milwaukee Railroad, upgraded from 'just another station along the line.' This was an important economic development as the railroad became the largest employer in town.
- Frame buildings on Seventh Avenue between 10th and 11th streets are replaced with two-story brick structures claimed to be fireproof. They housed businesses owned by four men: Joe Coenen, Wellington Kendall, R.D. Stephens and Benjamin H. Nott.

1884

- By March the Presbyterians had purchased land on Eighth Avenue and 12th Street where the First Presbyterian Church continues to hold services in the 21st century.
- Between 1884 and 1886 Marion became a full-fledged railroad town with an influx of workers.
- Jasper "Jap" Stouffer became manager of a new implement store on Seventh Avenue near 13th Street. In October 1884, W. Henry Halley bought the corner lot at Seventh Avenue and 13th Street for $1400 and operated a livery business from the barn on the property. In March 1886, Halley sold the property for $3,800 to Henry and George Etzel before the property was purchased as a library site in 1904. [Carnegie Library was completed in March 1905.]

1885

- J.C. "Jake" Davis, attorney and former mayor, remodels the former Presbyterian church building on 10th Street as his home and office.

1886

- Natural springs west of Marion are supplying Marion's celebrated spring water [and continued to do so for 66 years until 1952.] The properties on which springs are located are owned by J.C. Davis and Benjamin Bowman.
- The Post Office moved from the Smyth building south of the railroad tracks to the corner of the Daniels block.
- First band concert in City Square Park featured 10 musicians.

1887

- The former *Linn County Independent* became *The Marion Sentinel* with J.M. Smith, editor; the paper backed the Democratic Party.

1888

- The new Railway Depot that cost $15,000 began service in December.

1890

- The remodeled Biggs/Commercial Hotel building on Sixth Avenue was previously occupied by a bank and an abstract company. [The building was demolished in 1995 making way for the new library.]

1891

- The Order of Railway Conductors, organized in Marion, is called "Marion Division No. 268."
- A 17-minute ride between the friendly rival cities of Cedar Rapids and Marion became possible with the first electric cars on the suburban railway.
- The newly formed Old Settlers' Association held its first observance 2 October. Pioneers posed for a photograph on the steps of the Courthouse. [The meeting of old timers continues and, since 1996, has been part of Marion's Swamp Fox Festival held in early September.]

1892

- Namesake of Thomas Park (Richard "Uncle Dickie" Thomas) died at age 110. His widow and daughter reside in family home at Tenth Avenue and 18th Street. [The park was organized some 29 years later in 1921. Mary Thomas English, daughter, submitted the name, "Thomas Park." She and other Marion women worked to establish it.]

1893

- The first performance of the Cherry Opera Company—featuring the Misses Effie, Addie, and Jessie Cherry—takes place 20 January at the Daniels Opera House and nets $100 that the sisters said they would use "to find their missing brother."
- The first showing of Edison's Kinetoscope takes place at the Daniels Opera House.

1894

- Disastrous fire 8 August destroys the eastern three-quarters of the block on Seventh Avenue, opposite City Square Park, extending to the alley on 11th Street after the gas plant blew up. Extensive renovation eleven years earlier had included two-story brick buildings with common walls and tin roofs that were expected to be fireproof. They were not.

1898

- With the Spanish-American War in full swing, as many as 80 trains per day are being made up to carry freight coming into Marion.
- J.C. "Jake" Davis, according to his daughter (Carrie Davis Reichert) who wrote a brief history of Marion as she remembered it, bought the first car in town and sold it in 1898 to a Mr. Haskell in Cedar Rapids. It later turned up in the historical building in Des Moines.
- First "permanent" covered bandstand was built on the north side of City Square Park.

1899

- The Lincoln School, built in 1868, is getting an addition at Fifth Avenue and 12th Street.

1901

- In winter, the Marion Federation of Women's Clubs begin their campaign for a library building.
- The Milwaukee railroad began double-tracking the line between Sabula and Marion.
- A residential section of Eighth Avenue (called Pucker Street) is the first city street to be paved; livery stables along the avenue were still in vogue.
- A federal agency proclaimed Marion "the healthiest city in the U.S." The *Chicago Sunday Tribune* published a feature story suggesting that the pure spring water and a handy downtown railroad depot contributed to health. The government agency reported the average death rate (17.47 per thousand for cities with 1,000 or more people) far exceeded Marion's annual death rate of 1.4 per thousand.

Marion population at the time was more than 4,100.

•The first Marion Interstate Fair is held 12 and 13 September.

1902

•In February Mary Parkhurst is appointed librarian of Marion's first library, upstairs in building north of the park, between 10th and 11th streets.

•Asphalt paving is applied to Seventh Avenue between 10th and 13th streets, and 12th Street between Sixth and Eighth avenues.

1904

•The 14th annual reunion of Old Settlers' Association (P.G. Henderson, president) featured many speeches in City Park on 22 September. Special rates on all railroads were offered to facilitate attendance from around the area. Addresses by the Hon. R.G. Cousins of Tipton and Rev. Krome of Springville. "Ten-minute after-dinner" talks from more than 17 men included Daniel Coste, Robert Stinson, W.J. Brown, A.M. Secrist, S.W. Mentzer, Frank Hendricks, A.M. Flude, Frank Rogers, I.P. Bowdish, A.C. Burnett, James E. Bromwell, Captain Henry Sailor, C.S. Howard, D.E. Voris, Rev. Campbell, M.P. Smith, C.W. Bingham and others.

•Performance of "A Western Girl" 14 December benefits the proposed Library.

1905

•The Carnegie Library Building is dedicated on 6 March; a benefit sale for the Library netted $33.10.

•Fifth Avenue and 10th Street, site of the first Linn County jail, becomes site of the second Catholic Church.

•Double tracking west of Marion began. [By 1930, 25 years later, modern signaling and side tracks had made single tracks adequate, and by 1932 more than 100 miles of second track were torn up.]

1909

•The Library Board purchased a Remington typewriter for $100.

•Five of Marion's churches had been reproduced on a penny picture postcard to be used for communicating by mail.

•Samuel W. Durham died at age 92 in May. He was survived by five of his children. Two, Canfield Durham and Louise Durham, live in Marion. His wife, Ellen Wolcott, died in 1901. Durham migrated on horseback into Iowa in 1839 and surveyed "large portions of northern and northwestern Iowa and Minnesota under government contract." He was a large landowner who spoke lovingly about early pioneer days.

1910

•Mike Cira operated a confectionery on Seventh Avenue where Danish Maid Bakery later located.

1913

•The Marion Federation of Women's Clubs gave money for library books.

1914

•The City Council voted to pave eight more blocks of city streets with brick.

•A $25,000 fire at the lumber yard at 13th street and Seventh Avenue resulted in some damage to the Carnegie Library on 15 October.

1915

•Story reading program for school children began at the Library on 25 March.

•Big auto races scheduled for July 5 at the Interstate Fairgrounds.

1916

•In November, with no change in the tax levy to help raise funds, the Women's Federation voted to pay $70 on the $210 library lot debt. The following month the group paid off the debt with $147 proceeds from a home talent play presentation. The year was regarded as the most successful for the organization; its greatest accomplishments were buying the lot west of the Library for $1200 and improving the Cemetery League.

•It was reported that 176,977 automobiles are registered in Iowa.

•Mike Cira purchased the Dumont Building (now Kuba) for a grocery on Seventh Avenue opposite City Park. Previously the family worked in a store owned by Mrs. Cira's father on Seventh Avenue. [Cira's was last listed in the 1967 city directory.]

•A picture of the Pacific Limited train is available on a post card.

1917

•On 18 January, great library growth was noted with 16,218 volumes loaned, 477 new volumes added to the collection, and $1,559 spent for upkeep during 1916. A city tax levy expressly for the Library produced $1,695.84.

•A Chautauqua, held in Marion in May provided summer work for college students, and cultural entertainment and religious inspiration for families. The first Chautauqua was organized in New York State in 1874 by two men active in the Sunday school movement.

1918

•The Library closed during the winter to lower heating expense. Except for a half-hour each day (4 to 4:30 p.m.) when books could be exchanged, the library remained closed through January and February, the two coldest months of the year. Miss Pierce, librarian, attended book ordering and other matters from her home, and also made a complete catalog of the library collection.

•In July Miss Pierce held her first story hour of fairy tales for children at the library.

•Catherine Pierce resigned at the end of the year to accept her new position as librarian in Riverside, California. The Marion Federation group gave her a traveling bag and the Loyal Women's class of the Christian Church held a picnic supper at the home of Mrs. Fred Rowe in her honor. The Library Board said: "Miss Pierce will be greatly missed by the people of Marion and their good wishes go with her to her new work."

1919

•Lenna Huffman was named new librarian in February 1919.

•Andrew Carnegie died in April, 15 years after his grant made the Marion library possible.

•Three Marion residents died in the influenza epidemic.

•In June, plans for paving the Boulevard to Cedar Rapids were announced; the street railway tracks must be moved.

•A section of cement paving called "the seedling mile" is laid on the Lincoln Highway southeast of Marion—an initial step in rescuing motorists from Iowa mud.

•In the 6 November election, Marion lost the Courthouse to Cedar Rapids after putting up a good fight for 64 years to keep it at Linn County's first city.

•An ordinance proposing that movie theaters and Chautauqua in Marion be closed on Sundays was defeated when Mayor C.W. Biggs cast a vote to break the 3-3 tie.

•The treasurer reports approximately $20,000 on hand in the city treasury.

•Post 298 of the American Legion was organized at a meeting in Memorial Hall; Allen McElwain, named first commander. Initiation fee is to be one dollar with two dollar annual dues.

1921

•City leaders decided Marion will replace volunteer units with a city-operated fire department; paid nearly $10,000 for a 4-cylinder American LaFrance self-propelled apparatus. Elmer E. King was appointed first fire chief and reorganization was completed in September.

•Thirteen acres in southwest Marion are to be developed as a park. It was named Thomas Park to honor an early land owner.

•In August the Marion Federation of Women's Clubs' members served meals from Tuesday through Saturday at the fair to raise funds for the new park.

1922

•"Improvements" were made to the library according to news reports in August.

•Marion's second most destructive fire, at the corner of Seventh Avenue and 12th Street, took place 15 December. The fire hydrants were frozen and produced no water when firemen connected their hoses. Losses included uniforms and mementos of the famed Mentzer Drill Team that had been housed in the Mentzer Hose House. Damaged also were the C.E. Gordon grocery and Ed Sigfred store.

•Bond issue ($750,000) passed to fund a new courthouse to be built in Cedar Rapids on Mays Island between the Third and Fourth Avenue bridges over the Cedar River.

1923

•Old Settler (1839) Isaac N. Kramer died 23 February at age 90 leaving an unedited book manuscript about the county's early history. It was discovered 60 years later in state archives at Iowa City by his great-great grandniece (Jean Strong) and published in 1996 as *A Prairie Almanac, 1839 to 1919*, the eyewitness story about everyday life of pioneers as told by Isaac N. Kramer.

1925

- On 18 June, the city bid $1,200 at public auction for the Courthouse, but sale was not completed because two months later the city had insufficient general funds to pay for it. A proposal to levy two mills over 20 years to provide $20,000, the estimated cost for remodeling the building as a community center, was not favored by citizens.
- The Marion Country Club purchased the Fair Grounds along Indian Creek.

1926

- County supervisors passed resolutions granting City Square property to City of Marion with the stipulation that it always be "used exclusively for park purposes."
- L. O. Dickey purchased Clyde Martin's grocery that was previously Carl Reichert's and originally Mentzer's grocery.

1928

- Librarian Lenna Huffman lobbied the Lions Club in March for more support for the Library. As the fourth librarian, she had served 10 years thus far, received one small raise early on. She encouraged book donations, and proposed a new project to take books to and from shut-ins.
- In November, a children's story hour was held for classes from the grade schools.
- The Marion-Linn Chapter of the DAR (Daughters of the American Revolution) was formed.

1930

- American Legion Post #298 built a swimming pool adjoining Thomas Park; "one of the largest and best equipped in the state," according to Marvin Oxley.

1932

- City laborers who work on streets and the cemetery suffered a cut in wages from 40 cents to 30 cents an hour.
- A new Marion athletic field opened at 1st Street and Third Avenue.

1937

- Bus service between Marion and Cedar Rapids began on 3 November and the last day for the electric trolley was 10 days later.

1938

- The first office building constructed for the exclusive use as a Post Office is opened at Eighth Avenue and 11th Street; a WPA mural is part of the interior decoration.

1940

- On Saturday, 3 October, First Annual Corn Festival took place on Seventh Avenue, attracting thousands to exhibits and Thomas' Outdoor Stage Shows. The Library hosted a hobby show, supervised by the Marion Federation of Women's Clubs.
- In December, the Hiawatha trains of the Chicago, Milwaukee, St. Paul & Pacific railroad joined the premier Arrow trains serving Marion and other stops between Chicago, Omaha and beyond.
- S.P. "Lev" Leverich, former real estate man and town character, died in Marion.

1942

- Bill Reed Day is celebrated 12 September with a parade, speeches and banquet at Indian Creek Country Club. William N. Reed returns after winning fame as a member of the American Volunteer Group who flew with Chenault's Flying Tigers.

1946

- Ralph P. Young purchased *The Marion Sentinel* from the J.L. Papes family. Mr. Papes, named a Master Editor and Publisher by the University of Iowa and a journalism fraternity in the 1940s, owned the *Sentinel* for several decades.

1947

- *The Marion Sentinel* mounted a straw poll, "Should Marion citizens ask to be annexed to Cedar Rapids?" Voter response (1,916) defeated the issue with 76 percent opposing.

1948

- Rural school houses around county are reorganized. [Ten years later, after the June 1958 elections, the new Linn-Mar School District emerged.]

1957

- Dial telephone service comes to Marion.

1959

- New railway underpass is constructed at First Street and Seventh Avenue.
- Metta Whitcomb retires as library director in June.
- In November, voters approve a library addition.
- In December, the building that housed Marion's first courthouse on 10th Street is to be razed by

Murdoch Funeral Homes with space used for parking.

•Dickey's grocery became Bud Dickey's Dry Cleaning when he established the new business in the building that had housed grocery stores for almost 90 years.

1962

•Veterinarian Victor L. Klopfenstein and family moved to Marion. As mayor from 1988-2003, he worked with the City Council, administrators and the Marion Economic Development Corporation to advance Marion as both a commercial- and industrial-friendly city. He served on the city council before he was elected mayor.

1964

•Marion's first city manager, Pete Crivaro, was hired early in 1964 after growth brought challenges greater than the Mayor-Council government could handle without dedicated professional assistance.

•Merging with Cedar Rapids government was considered but not pursued.

•Residents approved a bond issue to build a new fire station at 600 Eighth Avenue; it has been in use since 1965 as Station Number 1.

•The new YMCA facility opens at Tenth Avenue and 31st Street.

1965

•A bond issue for developing Squaw Creek, a county park southeast of Marion, is approved.

•The new fire station is built at Eighth Avenue and 6th Street.

1966

•Robert Kennedy, aspiring Democratic nominee for president, draws a large crowd on his campaign stop at City Square Park.

1969

•Only one passenger train is leaving Marion in either direction (west to Omaha and east to Chicago) as American railroad service is being challenged by the versatility and speed of bus and airline services.

•After 31 years at its Eighth Avenue site, a new Post Office opens at Sixth Avenue and 11th Street.

1970

•Former Cedar Rapids Mayor Robert M.L. Johnson became Marion's third city manager.

•Marion's Chamber of Commerce became a division of the Cedar Rapids Chamber but the Marion office issues a monthly *Marion Report*.

•Marion's Fire Department created a Fire Prevention Bureau; firefighters are trained as Emergency Medical Technicians.

•A swimming pool, locker room and larger gym are added to the YMCA.

1971

•Amtrak spelled the end of passenger service through Marion. On 2 May the last regularly scheduled passenger train ran eastbound.

•Lincoln School building, dating from 1868, is being razed. Mentzer Elementary School is opened at Third Avenue, east of the football field.

1975

•Irving School is rededicated as Marion's Community Center.

1976

•Granger House, historic museum, opens to the public on 10th Street and Central Avenue.

1978

•Cable television is available in Marion.

•Armar Plaza Mall opens with Applegate's Landing restaurant as its first business.

•First National, Iowa's oldest national bank, opens at new location on Seventh Avenue and 3rd Street.

1980

•The Marion Library celebrates its 75th year by publishing a 19-page pamphlet, "History of Marion Carnegie Library 1905-1980" by Cecil G. Douglass.

•The last scheduled freight train left Marion on 1 March "with four engines, 51 cars, two snow plows and a caboose."

•On 4 March an eastbound train picked up the last cars and yard units operating between Marion and Savanna, Illinois. [A single track that served small businesses still relying on rail service was closed in 2002.]

•The Fire department added advanced paramedic emergency services during the eighties.

•Indian Creek Mall at 1st Street and Seventh Avenue has opened.

1984

•New police station is completed on Highway 151 East.

1986

•New swimming pool at Willowood Park is completed in northeast Marion (1855 35th Street).

1988

•The depot was torn down and its roof used on a pavilion in City Park. Bricks were cleaned and used in constructing the building.

•Marion Square Plaza, replacing many old store buildings, opens at Seventh Avenue and 11th Street.

1989

•Marion celebrates its sesquicentennial with a parade and festivities in City Square Park.

1990

•The Marion Depot Pavilion is opened in City Square Park through the efforts of many dedicated citizens.

•Marion continues celebrating its heritage that began in 1989 (sesquicentennial) with the Swamp Fox Festival honoring Marion's namesake, General Francis Marion of Revolutionary War fame. [Nearly 30 other American cities share the name of Marion.]

•The first female firefighter (Maureen Brown Boots) joins the Fire Department.

1991

•A second fire station (#2) on the east side became the fire department's new headquarters. More than 50 firefighters, men and women, volunteers and career personnel, protect the city.

•The *Marion Times* weekly newspaper begins publication five years after the *Marion Sentinel* ceased to publish.

1992

•The Balster Furniture Store closes after 68 years in service to Marion citizens. Balsters opened in 1924.

1993

•The first Marion Arts Festival is held in City Square Park.

•Devastating floods across the state did not spare Marion. Indian and Dry creeks flood many homes.

1995

•Construction begins on the new Library at Sixth Avenue and 11th Street.

1996

•In July the Marion Public Library opens. In November, Friends of the Marion Library open a used bookstore off the library lobby that is operated by volunteers; proceeds go to the library.

2000

•Marion Independent School District began its 140th year as the oldest school district in the county. With more than 2,000 students, the district employs 274 including 10 administrators, 5 supervisors, 96 classified (office workers, hot lunch people and others not otherwise categorized), 163 certified teachers. Twenty-eight percent of school revenues derive from local property taxes.

•George and Alyce Lowe donate 182 acres of farm land between North Tenth Street and Alburnett Road for a future Marion park complex. Lowe Park is planned for development in five phases and will be designed for use for the next 100 years. The gift of land extends for a mile along north Tenth Street and west to the Alburnett Road. [Phase I, Lowe Memorial Gardens, will encompass 15-acres. II, 37 acres, will be the Athletic Area. III, 15 acres for a Community Center. IV, 78 acres, Celebration Area, and V, 8 acres for a Meditation Retreat Center.] Total cost is estimated at nearly $12.9 million. A grant from Vision Iowa has been received for initial planning.

•The Marion Heritage Center, located in the former Baptist Church at Sixth Avenue and 10th Street, will be dedicated to educating the public about Marion's history.

2001

•A new post office opened in Marion on Highway 151 East.

2002

•In August two of the largest economic developments in Linn County were welcomed at Marion Commerce Park in east Marion. Cameron Ashley Building Products is a wholesale distributor of building materials; Legacy Manufacturing assembles and turns out oil pumps, delivery systems and accessories.

•Preliminary plans are advanced for the use of abandoned rail tracks through Marion for recreational purposes.

•The site for a new City Hall Complex is chosen on Highway 151 East; it was the location of Econofoods Supermarket that closed in 2004.

- The Pucker Street District on Eighth Avenue received recognition and is placed on the National Register of Historic Places. Three Eighth Avenue homes, individually, were also recognized as being of historic significance.
- The Sheets-Forrest-Draper Insurance Agency on 10th Street marked its 100th year of serving the community through times of prosperity and hardship since 1902.

2003

- Mayor Vic Klopfenstein announces he will not run for office again.
- Voters elect councilman John Nieland as mayor.

2004

- New city hall site is now slated for downtown, rather than in east Marion. Plans are not final.
- The Boyson families, supporters of Marion parks for many years, donate 14 acres in northwest Marion. Bruce and Robert Boyson presented the parcel on 22 June to the City Council. Located between West 14th Avenue and the southern edge of Boyson Road, the land is heavily wooded and "has potential for hiking and biking trails," said parks and recreation director Richard Fox. Cedar Rapids jeweler Adolph Boyson purchased the land in 1939 from the George A. Strong Estate.

Signs were placed at entrances to Marion in 2002. Above (right) Mayor Vic Klopfenstein and friends. At left center is Cedar Rapids Mayor Paul Pate.

SECTION THREE

MARION LIBRARY HIGHLIGHTS

1901 TO 2005

Miss Adeliza Daniels was a moving force in the push for a library building in Marion. This sketch, from a daguerreotype of her at age 25, was made for the library in 1980 by her great-niece, Mrs. Welzie H. Fones, Des Moines.

1928 Prominent Marion women were charter members of the Marion-Linn DAR. Among them: Mary Parkhurst, first librarian (left, back row); middle row: Grace Christie Koppenhaver, Gazette's Marion correspondent, 3rd from left; Bertha Owen, 2nd from right; front row: Mary Mentzer Hollingsworth, at left, became postmistress in 1937, and Adeliza Daniels, library promoter, center front. Other women are Ida Bowman, Nell Lothian, Mary Kendall, Alice Busby, Norma Romes, Maud Johnson, Mabel Gallivan, Alberta Sigfred, Effie Miller, Caroline Mentzer, Anne Hewett and Florence Christie Crew.

1901

•Miss Adeliza Daniels, daughter of early Marion pioneer family, is pursuing a library for Marion. She inspires Marion women's clubs to organize as a federation. Officers of the Marion Federation of Women's Clubs: Miss Daniels, president; Mrs. W.A. Dobson, Mrs. B.C. Busby, Mrs. C.H. Marshall, Mrs. Fred Olney (replaced the following year by Mrs. Harry Lathrop). Miss Mary Parkhurst is elected first librarian.

1902

•First library opens in the Owen Block, Seventh Avenue, second-floor room donated by E.J. Christie. The City Council names a board of trustees: Miss Daniels, Mrs. Dobson, Mrs. Busby, Mrs. Carl Owen, Miss Emma Tyler, E.I. Alderman, J.W. Bowman, Gary Treat and J.S. Alexander who is first board president.

1903

•On 30 March, Marion citizens vote on the library question. Result: 766 for, 123 against. Only seven women in the city's four wards vote no. [Women could not vote in national elections until 1920.]

1904

•*Western Girl*, a play, nets $33.10 to benefit the proposed library.

•Library Board votes to buy the corner lot at 7th Avenue and 13th street ($3,973) as the new library site. [C.E. Mitchell reduced his price by $200 requesting that amount be his contribution.]

•Mrs. Owen maintained a list of pledges ($150 to $5 range) from 30 people totaling $1,320 toward the purchase. Retired city engineer Ralph Mills (in a 2001 interview with Dr. Paul Orcutt and Voanne Hansen) recalls: "The library was originally started by a women's organization. Marion was a railroad town, kind of rough and tumble, and the ladies decided it was time to tame it and have something cultured. At that time, Andrew Carnegie, a Pittsburgh steel magnate, was giving communities like this the buildings for libraries with columns on each side of the entrance door and the tiled roof, just beautiful little buildings. I've seen them all over the country. They made application and sure enough they got Andrew Carnegie's group to give them the money to build this beautiful library building on the corner of 7th Avenue and 13th Street. It was an ideal location, close to town and available. The building is still standing there and you can still see those pillars."

GIFT OF MR. ANDREW CARNAGIE.
FREE TO THE PEOPLE.

Letter from Carnegie grants money for library in February 1903. Program celebrates opening of the new Carnegie Library in March 1905.

The Board of Trustees
of the
Free Public Library,
Marion, Iowa,
invite you to be present at the
Dedication of the Library Building,
March sixteenth, nineteen hundred and five,
two o'clock P. M.,
Methodist Church.

Program.

Invocation - - - - - - - - - - Rev. T. M. Evans
Music, - - - - - - - - - - - Male Quartette
      Report of the President of the Board.
Presentation of Federation Library to the City, - Mrs. B. C. Busby
Response, - - - - - - - - - C. H. Marshall, Mayor
Address, - - - - - - Rev. Robert Lincoln Campbell
Addresses, J. E. Bromwell, F. L. Anderson, D. E. Voris and G. E. Finch
Music, - - - - - - - - - High School Octette
What the Library is to the School, - - - - Miss Alice E. Duffy
Song—America, - - - - - - - - - - Audience
Benediction, - - - - - - - - - Rev. A. D. Kinzer

   A public reception will be held in the Library building at the close of the above program, from 4:30 until 9 o'clock.

We are having beautiful
weather. Best [...]
to all. Belle Davis.

we think it quite a nice
building, quite an improvement on the
rooms we had when you were here.

Marion, Ia.
Nov. 14"

Dear Edith.
The Library
has the
first Post
Cards. So
will send
you one
to [...]

MARION PUBLIC LIBRARY.

First postcard of library, written by Belle Davis, is postmarked 1905.
Original floor plan, Carnegie building

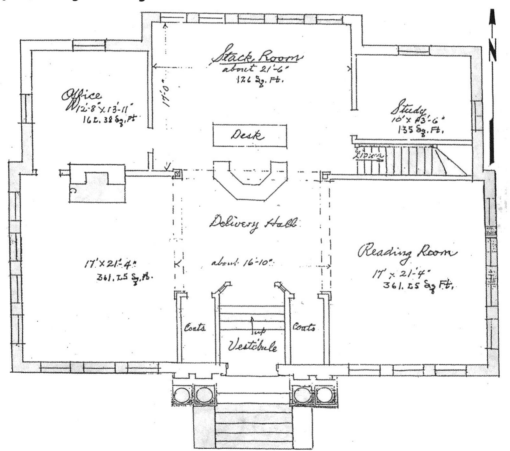

Stack Room
about 21'-6"
126 Sq. Ft.

Office
12'-8" x 13'-11"
162.38 Sq. Ft.

Study
10' x 13'-6"
135 Sq. Ft.

Desk

17' x 21'-4"
361.25 Sq. Ft.

Delivery Hall

about 16'-10"

Reading Room
17' x 21'-4"
361.25 Sq. Ft.

Coats

Coats

up

Vestibule

Miss Mabel Alexander, daughter of a Marion druggist, becomes the second librarian in 1909. (1941 photo reprinted with permission ©2004, *The Gazette*, Cedar Rapids, Iowa.)

Staff and volunteers, in front of library, c. 1915

•Library Board hires Cedar Rapids architectural firm, Dieman & Fiske, for a $9,898 fee. Contractor A.H. Conners begins work on 7 September 1904, five days after being selected.

1905

•On 16 March, dedication program for the Marion Free Public Library is held at the Methodist Church. Mayor C.H. Marshall accepts the library building on behalf of the city.

•In 1905, with city population at 4,138 and 1,105 books in the library collection, book circulation totaled 8,400.

1906

•Trees are purchased for planting on library grounds; $10 price will be paid later.

1910

•Librarian Alexander introduces a system allowing teachers to distribute books to students in the Marion schools. The plan to entice students into the library was later declared a success.

1911

•Repairs to the library roof are needed; the Board requests a 2 ½ mill levy for operating costs.

1912

•Katherine Pierce succeeds Mabel Alexander as librarian. [Miss Alexander is later employed by the Detroit Public Library.]

•City steam heat is installed in the library at a cost of $250.00.

1913

•The City Council levies a 2 mill tax for the Library.

•In November, the Marion Federation of Women's Clubs donates money for book purchases.

On 13 February 1919, Lenna M. Huffman succeeds Katherine Pierce as librarian.

Library provides background for high school graduates Arlene Atz (Smith), Fern Dodge (Kramer) in front, and friends in 1920.

Metta Whitcomb succeeds Lenna Huffman as librarian in 1932. She served as apprentice and assistant librarian the previous 18 years.

1914

•Fire that destroys a nearby lumber yard results in more than $200 damage to library fixtures and books, windows, curtains, casings, spouting, cornice and woodwork.

•Library's name is changed from Marion Free Public Library to Marion Carnegie Library.

1915

•Heat bill from Iowa Railway & Light Co. is $55.80 per month.

•A boulevard light is placed in front of the library; the $25 cost paid from city tax for street lights.

1916

•The Board agrees to purchase the lot west of the library building to enlarge the grounds; approves a bill for $13.15 for grading and seeding the lot. Ralph Mills recalls: "The ladies got ahead of a businessman who wanted to start a farm machinery business on that property."

•Charity teas 5 October benefit library project.

•In November, Women's Federation moves to pay $70 toward $290 debt for library lot; in December they paid off the balance with proceeds from a home talent play.

•The year 1916 sees great growth for the library with 477 new volumes added.

•Circulation totals 16,218. A city tax levy produces $1,696; 23 rural borrowers have cards.

1917

•The local American Red Cross chapter receives permission to use the library auditorium.

1918

•World War One ends on 11 November.

1919

On 13 February, Lenna M. Huffman succeeds Katherine Pierce as librarian.

1921

•On 28 April, library catalog is being updated.

1922

•Among the books added to the library collection is Iowa author Herbert Quick's *Vandemark's Folly.*

Painting of Andrew Carnegie, benefactor

1923

•On 10 January, librarian reports previous quarter increases in books loaned (2,000 more) and borrowers by 88.

•The Marion School Board requests use of the library for classrooms while the new high school is being completed, but a letter from the Carnegie Institute says granting the request would be "In violation of the Carnegie agreement."

1925

•Newspaper reports more than 25,000 books circulate to 1,500 Marion residents and 50 area people. City residents have 1,609 library cards.

1926

•Emery Miller, banker at First National, is appointed to the Library Board in January 1926 following the sudden death of bank president James W. Bowman (1862-1925). At the time of his death, Bowman was president of the Library Board and was associated with the Library for 21 years from its beginning.

1928

•Librarian Lenna Huffman lobbies for more library support and encourages book donations.

•A Children's Story Hour called "Tell Us a Story" is promoted.

DEPRESSION ERA BEGINS
1930

•Librarian Huffman reports "decided increases in circulation of books for home use (27,330)" up 1,583 from previous year, more than 42 percent by children.

1932

•Economic crisis prompts city officials to reduce the library allowance. Estimated income for 1933 is $1500. Librarian's salary is reduced to $40/month from $50. A cap of $18/month is placed on the assistant librarian whose hourly pay is 20 cents; she will work 90 hours to earn $18.

•Gift books help the library keep its collection current; on 26 April at a special meeting the board adopts a three-day week: open Tuesday, Thursday and Saturday afternoons; evenings as usual.

•The Marion Federation of Women's Clubs agrees to finance upkeep of library grounds by hiring unemployed men (under Reconstruction Finance Corporation, RFC) for spring cleanup.

1935

•On 3 July, a 3-mill tax levy is approved. Expenditures total $2,770. Remodeling steam heat plumbing cost $340.

•In November, on Andrew Carnegie's 100th birthday and the library's 30th, an oil painting of the benefactor is presented to the library. The program includes a speech by Earl Brockman and an old and new book display by Mrs. O.M. Carson and veteran book man, O.G. Waffle.

•State Library Examiner decrees all library funds be placed with the city treasurer in a library account. Funds include: $186.73 in First National checking; $1,726.82 in First National savings, and $1,131.41 in a Marion Savings Certificate. All $3,044.96 is duly transferred. In December, books are loaned to men in the Civilian Conservation Corps (CCC) encamped in Marion.

1936
• Roof repair by Kendall Hardware totals $35.11.

1937
• With $1,800 budgeted for the year, the Board authorizes $50 for purchasing fiction and young people's books.

1938
• Iowa Electric Company, discontinuing steam service next year, offers to pay $775 to Cedar Rapids Gas for installing a gas-fired steam boiler; the Board accepts.

1939
• The Musical Literary club presents Library with the book, *Musical Iowans: a Century of Music in Iowa*, published by the Iowa Federation of Music Clubs in observing the Territorial Centennial celebration of 1938.
• Librarian Whitcomb reported in May that the collection contained 10,627 books, 37 magazine and four newspaper subscriptions; the Library had loaned 31,208 volumes to 1,730 registered borrowers.
• New shelves are added to the adult reading room (under the south windows) for magazines and pamphlets.
• Many community groups and clubs, including Camp Fire Girls, use the auditorium.

1941
• "Forward with Books" is theme of Book Week Nov. 2-8 for that event's 22nd anniversary.

1944
• New books show wartime interests: John Hersey, *A Bell for Adano* (allied soldiers in Italy); *The 10 Commandments*, 10 writers create essays on the commandments showing how Hitler broke all moral laws; *What to Do with Germany*, by Louis Nizer and *Here Is Your War*, Ernie Pyle.

1947
• The library is voting site for an all-city straw poll regarding annexation of Marion to Cedar Rapids.

Carnegie Library, 1938

1948

•Ruth Mills (wife of Ralph Mills, city engineer) moves to Marion from Adel, Iowa and is soon hired as library assistant.

RECOVERING FROM DEPRESSION YEARS
1952

•Librarian Metta Whitcomb is permitted to spend $150/year for books without contacting the book committee.

•A newspaper headline reports the library loaned 30,881 books during 1952.

•The Library is displaying a Civil War flag (34 Union stars) from former resident Alice Fernow, now of Massachusetts.

1953

•Sandblasting by C.R. Jeffries Co., Des Moines, is completed in August on the pillars and other stonework at front of the Carnegie Library building.

1955

•The Marion Federation of Women's Clubs hosts the 50th Library Anniversary event.

1957

•The Board proposes converting part of the basement into a Children's Room. Mrs. Richard Marsh is hired as children's librarian at $75/month.

1958

•Eight libraries in Linn County circulate 792,626 books in 1958, according to *Cedar Rapids Gazette*, 22 March 1959. Marion Library accounts for more than 50,000.

1959

•In July, building expansion plans (addition and equipment) are presented with petition for an election on an $80,000 bond issue. This passed in 1959.

Miss Whitcomb (left) and Mrs. Mills in new children's room with Carol Voss, Jon Stanek and Karen Lucas in 1957.

O.O.P. club members present a portable record player for children's room use in 1957. From the left: Esther (Mrs. Hugh) Gordon, Sara Nott and Ruth Marie (Mrs. Ron) Schueler.

After nine years as assistant librarian, Ruth Mills (above) in 1959 replaces retiring Metta Whitcomb who headed the Library for 27 years. A tea honoring Miss Whitcomb is held at the home of Faye (Mrs. Kenneth) Murdoch.

1960

•Board acknowledges "sub-standard" conditions in the adult section. WW I titles and other little-used collections are stored in the basement. Of three plans considered, the 3rd is approved. [Plan #1 included no additional seating or shelving; #2 doubles size of stack room with mezzanine floor and four-foot stairway; seating remains at 36; #3 addition to north side of library with an assembly hall seating 200 on lower floor.] Budget request: $14,556/year.

•Out-of-town borrowers are asked to pay a two dollar annual fee.

1961

•The two-story with basement addition, nearly doubling space, opens in April 1961 and circulation increased dramatically to 105,052 for the year.

•Mrs. Mills reports most popular book in 1961: *To Kill a Mockingbird* by Harper Lee, with William L. Shirer's *Rise and Fall of the Third Reich* second in popularity.

Photos to right, from top down of Carnegie Library. Remodeled checkout area in 1961, Mrs. Clara Folkers at work. Mezzanine and study area, north side, new addition. Exterior, new addition, from northeast.

Oxley's original [five] volumes are preserved inside cabinet; bound copies (on top) are for patron use.

•In June, remodeled Children's Room is ready; hours will be 6:30 to 8:30 p.m. beginning in September.

1963

•Bookcase with locking doors, from the Marion-Linn Chapter of the Daughters of the American Revolution (DAR), exhibits the five-volume *History of Marion* by Marvin Oxley (left). Books and bookcase now kept in reference area of the new library.

1964

•County library system being considered is postponed due to lack of funds.

•Marion library budget is $20,110.

•Anita Kemper resigns from the Library Board to become children's librarian.

1966

•The contract for county library service is approved with a $29,005 proposed budget.

•On average, 90 children attend story hours at the Marion Library each week.

Library employee Mrs. Ellen Bateman tries one of new chairs for patrons in 1963 *(Marion Sentinel* photo).

Library director, Edith "Bobbi" Duss, (left) with assistant librarian Barbara Penn in 1969.

Marion, Iowa
1980

Title page of 75th anniversary booklet

Carnegie Library, 1980

• Annual budget is set at $24,740.

1967

• The county card fee is raised to $5/year.

• Library receives $1,000 from the Phoebe Mentzer Lindquist Estate (Amherst, Massachusetts) honoring her mother, Mrs. Elza Mentzer. The money is to be used for books and articles on the history of Marion.

1969

• New library director Edith "Bobbi" Duss succeeds Ruth Mills who retired. Library budget is set at $38,410.

1970

• Emery Miller, after serving 44 years, is replaced on the Library Board by the new mayor.

1971

• Board considers purchasing air conditioner until they learn the entire building requires rewiring to accommodate it.

1972

• Board notes that children's circulation decline is less than decrease nationwide.

1973

• The City Pride award for landscaping program at the library is given to Mayor C.W. Bullis in January; it is the only award given outside of Cedar Rapids.

• Revenue Sharing funds revive interest in a library improvement program. Architects develop long-range plan.

1974

•In August, the $79,260 remodeling program, including elevator and air conditioning, is nearly complete.

1975

•Board considers, with County Supervisors, providing library service to rural residents.

•A new summer activity hour is offered in the children's room for 1st through 3rd grades with Mrs. Katie Bond, volunteer, directing.

1980

•Library celebrates 75th anniversary. Cy Douglass, former *Marion Sentinel* editor, wrote 19-page history of the library.

1981

•Creative Arts Council funds mural by elementary students in Marion and Linn-Mar schools, supervised by Marjory Jensen, art instructor. Mural was painted on library wall inside east entrance.

Gail Landy (above) replaces Bobbi Duss who retired as library director in 1983.

1983

•Women attending the Fifth Annual Library Trustees' Workshop on 30 April included: Marcella Hay, Voanne Hansen, Dolores Rose, Rene Kincheloe and Molly Andersen of Marion; Ellen Steele, Central City, and Shirley Henry, librarian from Hiawatha.

1984

•Board discusses need for roof repair.

•Women's Club gives $200 for children's books.

1985

•Board approves purchase of an Apple computer, printer and software program.

1986

•The Marion Library is offering a summer film program (June-August) along with its annual summer reading program (June and July) and a program for pre-schoolers.

•Library is named beneficiary of $5,000 in will of Monticello woman, Anna Rafter Henak.

•The first coin-operated copying machine is installed for patron use.

1987

•In February Board receives $1,426 for history books from the Gretchen Mentzer Estate. Miss Mentzer, a Marion native, taught Spanish and history in the Marion schools for many years.

•Gail Landy leaves director's position; moves to New Hampshire.

Susan Kling named Carnegie Library Director in May 1987.

•In May Board approves county contract for providing rural library services. In six months 100 new county families register for cards.

•The Marion Carnegie Library held a book sale 24 and 25 July of adult and children's materials (books, magazines and records).

• Family Night program is held in September with celebrity readers.

• Holiday open house features library's collection of holiday craft and cook books.

• Interior of library is painted and work room carpeted. Board begins study of future space needs.

1988

• All borrowers are asked to renew their registration; new cards are issued in April, updating the patron list.

• In October, the library participates in a Fire Extravaganza Parade with float whose theme was, "Books Warm the Heart."

• Planning group first meets to develop a Friends organization.

• In November new carpeting is installed on main floor. With library closed for a week, staff packs up all books for storage in the basement so shelves can be moved. As carpeting is laid, staff works in balcony weeding nonfiction collection; 6,000 books are withdrawn.

1989

• In January, Friends of the Marion Library group organizes; by May, 48 paid members are on board.

• Adult summer reading program is offered for first time.

• Cox Cable offers video equipment along with a collection of videotapes. This is an important gift because heretofore the Board had voted 5-4 against a video collection.

(Top) Outdated and worn nonfiction books withdrawn from library collection in 1988 make way for new books.

(Middle) Staff has little wriggle space in workroom.

(Bottom) Library float prepared by O.O.P Club (dedicated library supporter) wins award, 1989 Sesquicentennial parade.

At its 9 January meeting, the Board votes (5 to 4) to accept this gift and to purchase additional video tapes.

•Gift of $106,000 from the Jeanne R. Bowdish Estate is announced in March. Money is invested in CDs; interest from the bequest used to fund many of the consultants hired to help with building project.

•Susan Kling presents a building report to the Library Board in June; the Board directs it be sent to the City Council. Board president Vo-anne Hansen appoints a long-range planning committee.

•Library participates in Marion's Sesquicentennial Celebration September 1989 by opening, on Sunday afternoon, with displays about the city's history.

•Friends obtain the necessary 600 petition signatures to place the book levy on November's election ballot. The levy ($.04 on each $1,000 assessed value) passes by an 80 percent "yes" vote to help purchase materials.

•In October a fax machine is added to library services.

•Library solicits and receives proposals for the Space Needs Assessment. At 13 November meeting, the Board hires library building consultant David Smith with a fee cap of $6,800.

1990

•New carpet is laid in balcony and the lower level in January.

•Fiscal year 1990-91 sees $10,000 decrease in county funds.

•New service for patrons is called Quick Picks. Best sellers purchased for this special collection are not placed on reserve list. Books circulate for 10 days only with no renewals "to have some current best sellers in the library when people come in."

Carnegie Library in its 85th year

•Board member Llewellyn "Boo" Balster obtains use of six parking spaces for library staff from manager of a neighbor building (across 7th Avenue).

•Staff workroom is expanded in March.

•In April, Library celebrates 85th birthday during National Library Week.

•Family Night (Spooktacular) at the Community Center attracts 800 on 29 October.

1991

•Friends initiate a book discussion group in January that continues annually; sponsored by Humanities Iowa.

•The City Council includes library as a goal in its action plan.

•On 25 March, a bomb explodes in the book drop; repairs to windows and roof and replacement of book drop cost $5,567.85.

•In May library conducts a community telephone survey with volunteers trained by Frank Magid.

•Summer reading program attendance increased over the past 15 years with the help of Marion merchants.

•Site evaluation committee is established with library board, library and city staff. The committee evaluated Mentzer Elementary School on West Third Avenue as a potential library site.

•Public forum is held in September to discuss potential library sites. The Library Site Selection committee meets several times; each committee member evaluates 24 sites and six are considered possible.

•By 1 November, volunteers are regularly working 46.5 hours weekly in clerical, shelving, shelf reading, processing and special projects. Staff member Nancy Simpson is in charge.

Volunteers Voanne Hansen and Shirlee Mercer weed books in fiction collection, main floor.

1992

•In March, Library Site Committee recommends block south of City Square Park location.

•Friends two-day book sale nets $3,000; Friends request storage space in new library.

•Brown Healey Stone and Sauer, architects, submit draft of Site Location Study.

•Board meets with City Council in July to discuss site and architect's report.

•Compact discs (CDs) are placed in circulation.

•Architects present report on three possible library sites: vacant lot south of Longfellow School on Eighth Avenue; land on 10th Street south of historic Granger House, and the block south of City Square Park.

•Board sponsors public hearing in September.

•Board recommends block south of City Square Park location in October.

•The Board presents recommendations to the Council in November; Council defers decision.

•Board forms Fund Raising Planning Committee in December.

1993

•Barbara Penn, long-time library assistant, retires.

•In January Cheryle Mitvalsky, Kirkwood Community College, presents seminar for the Board on a major gifts campaign for the building project.

Children's Librarian Jean Hampson and husband, George, assess damage to bombed book return in 1991. Reprinted with permission © 2004, *The Gazette*, Cedar Rapids, Iowa.

•In March Board recommends fund raising feasibility study; hires Renaissance Group, Inc. to conduct it.

•In April Certificate of Accreditation by the state is presented to Board President Harry Baumert and Mayor Klopfenstein. Marion is among 62 of Iowa's 528 public libraries to earn accreditation in 1993.

•In May, Council passes resolution supporting Library building project.

•Board hires building consultant Julie Huiskamp in August to develop a building program statement.

•In December the National Register of Historic Places listing for the Carnegie Library building is approved by the state and submitted to the National Park Service.

1994

•In January Board hires Renaissance Group, Inc. to continue work on Capital Campaign and Brown Healey Stone & Sauer as building architects. Consultant recommends campaign goal of approximately $2 million.

Farmers State Bank executives present $100,000 check for the new library building fund in September 1994. From left are Clair Lensing, Library Director Susan Kling and Morris Neighbor.

•In February Stephen and Nancy A. Miller pledge $650,000 for the new library building.

•The Hall-Perrine Foundation made a $600,000 grant in April.

•Soliciting for gift pledges continues from February to April before special bond election is prepared.

•Voters pass the bond issue in May for $1.975-million by a 74.3 percent vote.

•In September, City Council accepts bid for sale of Carnegie building.

•Nine properties on the new library site are being acquired; another $68,000 for funding is yet to be raised.

•Architect completes building design, May-December. Community Fund Raising Campaign continues to December.

1995

•Sign contract with Cedar Rapids Public Library for use of its on-line catalog in January.

•Demolition bid awarded to Zinser Demolition; work to begin by 31 January.

•The capital fund raising campaign reaches its goal in February; final

Councilman Frank Reynolds congratulates director Susan Kling on bond issue success at a celebration party at her home.

amount raised: $2.3 million.

•Construction bids come in under budget; contracts awarded to low bidders: Garling Construction, Modern Piping, Speer Electric.

•Groundbreaking ceremony, 20 March.

•Roush Products and the new Library Foundation sponsor a celebration dinner at the Longbranch.

•In July library is designated as pilot site for ICN classroom (Iowa Communication Network).

•Roofer and masons begin work in September.

•Receive bids for library furnishings in October; contracts awarded to low bidders.

•In November *Cedar Rapids Gazette* donates a computer and software featuring the Nation Job Network (nationwide job openings).

1996

•Interior plumbing and electrical work continues in January with scheduled completion date of 1 May 1996.

•Interior painting is underway in February.

•On 21 March, 300 attend Library Foundation Sneak Preview.

•Work continues on interior painting and wall papering.

(continued on page 91)

(top) Old county jail on 11th St. makes way for library facility. (middle) House on 5th Avenue is demolished. (bottom) Old hotel building is razed at 6th Ave. and 11th St.

88

(top) Northwest corner of new library building shows construction progress.
(bottom) Framework for new building outlines tall window frame overlooking lobby area.

Checkout area, February 1996.

Reference area, April 1996.

Steel shelving awaits materials in May.

Brigade gathers outside for ceremonial transport of books from Carnegie to the new building on Sixth Ave.

Mayor Klopfenstein locks old library door on 23 June 1996, ending ninety-one years of free library access and service at 1298 Seventh Ave.

Interior doors and locks installed.

•Ceramic tile completed in two of four bathrooms.

•By April 1996 contractors are finishing work. Walk-through scheduled for 13 May.

•Iowa Electronics wins computer bid. Steel shelving delivered and installed in May.

•Colored glass windows installed. Work on lobby continues.

•The wet spring delays site work that continues into June.

•New library building is turned over to Library Board and City on 17 June.

•Install public and staff work stations and computers.

•Ceremonial closing of Carnegie Library with silent auction and book brigade takes place 23 June. Items sold net $7,125.

•Library Movers of America transport library materials, furniture and supplies 24-27 June.

•First three weeks in new building are spent settling in and training staff on new computer system. Cedar Rapids Public Library staff is very helpful.

•On opening day, 22 July, Library opens at 6 a.m. WMT-AM Radio and Burger King sponsor breakfast in the City Park Pavilion. McDonald's and WMT-FM Radio sponsor a lunch in the park.

•Grand Opening is held at 11 a.m., 24 August, with nearly 300 attendees. A thousand red

Paul Wieck, Dysart, Grand Master of the Masons' Grand Lodge of Iowa, seals Library cornerstone on 11 May at ceremonies conducted by the Masons. Since ancient times, the ritual for cornerstone placement favored the northeast corner symbolizing source of light and dawn of civilization. Reprinted with permission © 2004, *The Gazette*, Cedar Rapids, Iowa.

(1996 continued)

and blue "engineer" bandanas are distributed during the day. Receive $10,000 gift from the Hall-Perrine Foundation for purchasing additional library materials in honor of Susan Kling.

•Participate in Swamp Fox Children's Library parade on 7 September 1996.

•One hundred attend Friends program: "Yup, Nope and Why Midwesterners Talk That Way," 9 September.

•The Friends plan to use their space in the lobby for a bookstore.

•Nationally known storyteller David Novak comes to celebrate new library 14 September.

Ribbon-cutting at new library, five people in center, from left: Harry Baumert, library board president; Nancy A. Miller, benefactor; Susan Kling, director; George Lowe, building committee chair, and Mayor Vic Klopfenstein.

(above) **Inside the Library on opening day, a few of the patrons who checked out 3,789 items.**

Harry Baumert receives Trustee of the Year Award from fellow Board member Voanne Hansen (left) who accepted the award for him at the Iowa Library Association (ILA) annual meeting. At right is Board member and former school superintendent, John Messerli.

•Library Board President Harry Baumert receives Iowa Library Association (ILA) Trustee of the Year Award at October Board meeting.

•Library Director Susan Kling is elected vice-president/president-elect of ILA.

•Friends' book store off the library lobby opens 1 November with Marilyn Phelps in charge. Volunteers plan to keep store open 36 hours/week.

•Bequest of $4,836 received from Vaughn estate is placed in Memorial Fund.

November 1996, Friends bookstore opens. From left, three members of the Friends Board: Gerry Burkart, Marilyn Phelps, Voanne Hansen (Library Board liaison to the Friends) and Nancy A. Miller.

•Library Foundation hosts "Sunday Supper at the Library" on 3 November.

•Receive ICN Distance Learning Classroom equipment.

•In December Library staff receives training on ICN classroom equipment.

•Tom Aprile's sculpture "Tumbleread" is installed in the library; construction materials are brick, tile and wood.

•Legislative reception is held on 2 December.

•First six months in new library: 9,130 new borrower cards issued; 159,169 circulation (205,000 for all of fiscal 1996).

1997

•In January, a six-month statistical report on the library reveals: meeting room use, 705; computer lab use, 594.

•The library web page joins the City of Marion website.

•Law Chek, Ltd., of Cedar Rapids, presents library with a computer and legal software.

•Trees Forever contributes $1,000 for trees on library site.

•In July a reciprocal delivery system between Marion and Cedar Rapids libraries is initiated.

Marion's Bike Patrol celebrates opening of their downtown post in 1997 at the library. Two patrol officers are Jim Teahen (in front), Lance Miller, back row left. Police Chief Harry Daugherty is third from left. Others are Mayor Klopfenstein, Susan Kling and Marion Chamber of Commerce ambassadors.

•July first-year observance features celebrity storytellers: Mayor Klopfenstein, Iowa Senator Mary Lundby and Iowa Representative Rosemary Thomson for 200 children and parents.

•First-year sales for the Friends Bookstore (Nov. '96- Nov. '97) total $16,797.

•The Marion Police Department is stationing two bicycle patrol officers in the library with a small study room as their office.

•In September Library gets unlimited Internet access through the Cedar Rapids Public Library for $5,000/yr.

•Marion Library is one of 127 Iowa libraries to receive three-year accreditation from the State Library of Iowa.

•A software module allowing notification of patrons about overdue materials or on-hold materials saves time of library staff.

•Friends provide $3,000 for purchase and planting of flowering trees on the grounds.

•City of Marion receives All-Star Certificate from the Iowa League of Cities for public/private cooperation on the library project.

•The Library's Internet home page goes online.

•Board and staff set library's primary service goals: to provide popular materials and maintain a children's and young adults' collection. Secondary goals: to provide reference services and serve as a community center.

1998

•Director Susan Kling begins one-year term as president of the Iowa Library Association.

•Library Board votes, after a 90-day trial period, to continue service by Unique Collection Agency, to recover overdue fines and retrieve overdue materials. Previously $4,397 was collected and materials valued at $2,964 returned.

•In April a luncheon honors 97 volunteers for 2,856 hours contributed in the past year.

•Library receives $4,500 grant from the State Department of Cultural Affairs; a 13 August

Marlys Maske retires in January 1998 after 25 years of service to the Library.

1999 concert by the Boland-Dowdall Duo is scheduled.

•Painting by Fred Easker (North County Fields) is installed in the children's area. The Marion O.O.P. Club commissioned the work.

•Two used Pentium computers, given by Toyota Motor Credit Corp., will be used in the office and at the Information Desk for accessing the Internet.

•In September, Susan Kling demonstrates the Iowa Communication Network (ICN). In 1997, Marion was among the first of 40 public library installations state wide. ICN accesses information from government agencies, universities, colleges and public and private schools while saving travel time and fuel.

•Barnes and Noble Booksellers give Library a display table for exhibiting book collections and encouraging checkout of materials.

•"Lowe Meeting Rooms" sign above door honors library supporters George and Alyce Lowe.

•Board accepts Friends' offer to purchase paintings by Peter Thompson titled "Flute and Guitar" of the Boland-Dowdall Duo, and "Blues Men" depicting Bryce Janey and Merrill Miller. All are Marion area residents.

Husband and wife John Dowdall and Jan Boland are featured in painting by Peter Thompson (Flute and Guitar). Hung in the meeting room, the painting is a gift from the Friends.

"The Midnight Arrow" painting shows the passenger train that operated between Chicago and Omaha with Marion as one of its stops. Donors are Joyce and Howard Parks honoring her parents, John B. and Nellie Fosdick. Mr. Fosdick served many years as engineer on the Milwaukee line. Artist: Wendell Mohr. Painting is in reference section of library.

1999

•A bronze statue, "Bookworm," is presented to the library by Bert and Sue Katz in memory of Sue's son, Louis Rosenbaum. This inspired the M.J. Murray family to give a matching sculpture, "Bookworm II." The two sculptures outside the south library entrance depict a boy and a girl reading.

•The Metro Library card, introduced in June, can be used in the three Metro libraries—Cedar Rapids, Hiawatha and Marion.

•Iowa's first lady, Christie Vilsack, visits the library in July. She is promoting a new state-funded program, "Enrich Iowa—Fund Libraries." The Marion Library will receive $5,000.

•Bert and Sue Katz give $25,000 to the Library Foundation, funding several years of the summer reading program for children and young adults.

•The first computer shut-down occurs 13 July 1999.

•Councilwoman Mary Lou Pazour suggests the library have a "Christmas in July" tree featuring tags with magazine subscription prices; 18 subscriptions totaling $441.50 are received.

•The second Staff Development Day with Julie Huiskamp, library consultant, focuses on staff service to patrons, intellectual freedom and censorship.

•In November, entire computer network of 23 computers (5 new) is upgraded and memory added making the system operate faster and Y2K compliant.

•A "Spirit of Giving" tree generated donations of $482 that were used to purchase 26 audiovisual items. Thirty videos were also donated.

2000

•Director Kling brings idea of a Strategic Planning Process to the Board.

•Circulation is up 3,845 items over the previous May.

•The library's history book committee meets with Jean Strong in June; she is writing a library history for its centennial year 2005. Two board members and the director are gathering research for the book.

•Director Kling is working with Barb Feller, Granger House, and Lynda Waddington to develop a partnership grant for gathering historical data about Marion for presentation through a website.

•Revenue from Enrich Iowa totals $7,885 and is used for installing an additional ICN hub and three computer web interface catalog stations, additional shelving and a display rack for books

Library assistant Barb Ford retires in March 2000 after 31 years of service to the library. Ralph Mills recalls: "Shortly after taking over in 1959, Ruth [his wife] hired Barbara Ford as a high school girl. She was probably one of the best workers, a marvelous person in the library." Barb is shown above at the card catalog in the Carnegie building.

in CD and video in DVD format.

•The children's summer program ends 29 July with a total of 1,396,200 reading minutes by participants.

•In December, library receives $2,303 in donations used to purchase additional library materials.

2001

•In March, volunteers using the Farmers State Bank facilities help library staff telephone 300 Marion residents about their use and perception of the Library. The survey sample reveals: 52.7%

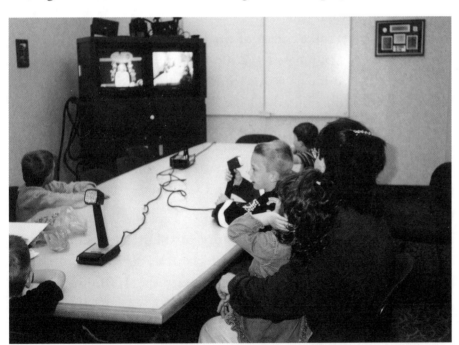

The ICN connection in the library's conference room allows residents to attend government or educational meetings without traveling away from Marion. ICN is a state wide system for state and federal agencies and distance learning for colleges, universities, public and private schools. Most frequent users are area home schooled students.

rate the Library as a 5, highest on a scale of 1 to 5; 27.9% rate it a 4.

•Library staff members march in the September Swamp Fox Parade pushing library carts adorned with signs proclaiming the library's services.

•A planning committee of local citizens begins study on the direction the library should take over the next three to five years.

2002

•A community-wide book discussion, Marion Reads, is inaugurated. Marion and Linn-Mar students and community members read "Whale Talk" by Chris Crutcher and attend discussion sessions. Sponsors include both school foundations, Friends of the Marion Library and the Marion Noon Lions Club.

•In April, library volunteers are honored at a luncheon and program. More than 60 volunteers contribute 1800-plus hours in the library from April 2001 through March 2002.

•In June, a Marion Arts Festival public art piece, "Spirit of America" is installed in the library.

•In December, the Library installs and implements VAM "VendPrint Access Management"—allowing patrons to sign up and manage the computer time they are allotted.

2003

•The library participates in the All Iowa Reads Program encouraging Iowans to read and discuss the same book. "Peace Like a River" by Leif Enger is chosen and Hills Bank buys 50 copies of the book for the library.

•A new library brochure is designed and printed with the help of board member, Jack Zumwalt, and Friends of the Library.

•Conversion to the new circulation and cataloging system, Sirsi iBistro™, is completed in one day in October; the library closed for installation and the beginning of staff training.

Jim Bouslog (right), Friends Foundation board member, presents $250,000 check to Doug Laird, representing owner of property that was site of the U.S. Post Office 1969-2001.

•Hills Bank sponsors a noon luncheon and book talk by local Marion people including Dr. Katie Mulholland, superintendent of Linn-Mar Schools, a library board member and several members of the library staff.

•Property east of the library, at 1101 Sixth Avenue, is purchased ($250,000) by Friends of the Library Foundation for future library parking. The Friends contributed $12,500. Other donations, large and small, helped acquire the land.

•Library participation in Christmas in the Park brings 400 children to the library for stories and ornament-making in December.

2004

•The 100-year history of the Marion Library and its city are the subject of a 100+ page book being published to commemorate the 100th anniversary event in March 1905.

2005

•Observances are planned to celebrate the 100th anniversary year of the Marion Library.

NEW LIBRARY FOR THE 2K CENTURY
Materials and Services Galore
and a Friendly, Helpful Staff

The Carnegie Library was stately; the new Marion Library is functional and has become a "front door" to the city. Equipped to meet the needs of a growing population, the new facility features on-site parking and a drive-up return for library materials. Local artwork, some recalling the city's past, enhances the ambiance. A dedicated staff plus larger budgets for library materials ensure that the changing needs of library users will be met in the years ahead.

Community programs for all ages and computers for accessing the world are available, along with the opportunity to purchase used books at the Friends' book store. A new service seeks to help busy citizens with access to a home computer; "Ask a Librarian" invites people to e-mail a query and a reference staff member responds with the answer. If you are not among the 875 people who visit every day, better check out The Marion Library.

Director Susan Kling's office provides a calm atmosphere for interacting with her staff. Here she confers with Jill Law (at left), circulation supervisor. Picture on wall was presented to the library by the O.O.P. club in memory of member Eva Fontaine, a dedicated library supporter. The annual budget for materials has increased from $35,000 in 1987 to $150,000 in fiscal 2004 and is supplemented by funds from Friends of the Library and the Library Foundation.

MEMORIES OF THE CARNEGIE CHILDREN'S DEPARTMENT

By Jean Hampson
Children's Librarian

The Children's Area in the new library includes books, videos, periodicals and a nine-section wooden train with seating and storage space for materials. The display case (foreground) for "sharing with children" was a gift from the Bond family in memory of Katie Bond, former volunteer in the children's department. The items on display here are from Linn-Mar art students to celebrate Youth Art Month, March 2004.

I have lived in Marion since 1961. I have always been a library user and in the fall of 1968 was hired as a "page" at the Marion Carnegie Library. I walked to the library every day after school to work for a few hours. My main jobs were shelving books and record albums, typing catalog cards on a manual typewriter, alphabetizing and filing those cards, checking out materials to patrons and counting and alphabetizing check out cards. I earned $.50/hour for my dream job.

At Carnegie, the Children's Room floor on the lower level was covered with linoleum tiles. We had no air conditioning and wore dresses to work. Both Anita Kemper, children's librarian, and her assistant, Leora Kriegermeier, worked part time. Each staff member worked one night in the adult section; the children's area was closed at night, and opened for afternoons at 12.

Two successful preschool story time groups met at the same time, each Thursday morning one for two and

1957. The new Children's Room at Carnegie Library, made possible by Marion club women and the Marion City Council, is ready for opening in the basement of Carnegie Library.

About 1961. Mary McCann, Children's Librarian in the `60s, proudly shares a book with Maureen Reynolds as young readers pursue other books in the Children's Room collection at Carnegie.

three year olds, the other for four and five year olds.

If anyone needed to use the rest room or retrieve a back issue of a magazine during hours the children's area was closed, they would unlock the door with a skeleton key, turn on the lights and go downstairs.

After graduating from high school, I continued at the library until I resigned to stay home and have a baby. We lived in Texas for three years while my husband was in the Navy; I returned to Marion with our two daughters in spring 1976 when he was sent overseas.

In December 1976, library director Edith "Bobbi" Duss phoned to ask if I wanted a job; Jan Gorman, the person who had replaced me, was leaving. I said "yes" and returned to work in January 1977. Children's librarian Leora Kriegermeier and a "page" were the other regular employees in the children's room. My 40-hour week included two evenings until 8:00. Nyle Ellson worked with me every Saturday.

During my five and one-half-year absence, the library

In 1968, Marjory King entertains at a story hour in the Children's Room at Carnegie Library.

In 1996, Jean Hampson reads to children at Carnegie Library in their dedicated basement room.

had a major renovation (carpeting, air conditioning and an elevator) and the staff had increased along with the open hours. When Leora retired, I became Children's Librarian.

Bigger changes came about when the Library moved into the new building in 1996. At Carnegie, with the Children's Room in the basement, we functioned almost as a separate entity with our own circulation desk and card catalog. Children's cards could be issued to five-year-olds. When a child came to borrow materials, we took his/her card from the file, stamped it with the due date, wrote the number of books being taken and re-filed the card. To check out books in the adult section, the child carried his card upstairs and returned it to us before going home.

When communication was required with the adult staff, we used a doorbell-like buzzer, alerting them to pick up the telephone receiver. Employees in both children and adult sections manually wrote up "fine cards" for overdue materials. We listed

Clifford, the Big Red Dog, keeps watch as small library users select materials to take home. Special programs include weekly preschool story times. Below, storyteller Julie Lammers captivates her audience at the new library.

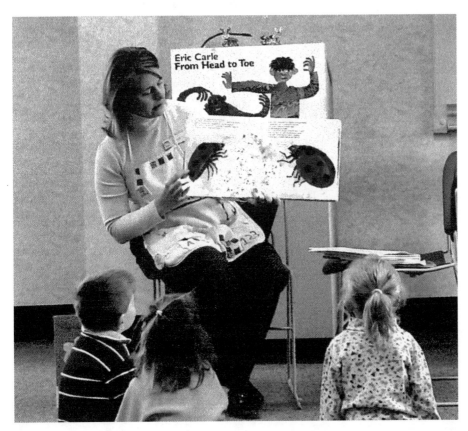

items by title, date due, date returned and attached it to the library card. Each night before closing, we took our fine money and daily circulation count upstairs.

In the new building, the circulation and catalog systems are automated, eliminating time spent filing catalog cards, writing on book cards, counting and filing everything by hand. We don't miss those daily chores.

Many things changed during my 26 years with the library, but the library's main purpose has not. We serve the people of Marion and surrounding areas with materials (now in many formats) to provide enjoyment, entertainment and learning. Many longtime users, children when I began, now bring their own children to use the library.

PARKING LOT ENTRANCE

Colored glass circles atop these south windows (right) cast multicolored shadows into the library. The circles represent wheels of the trains that once frequented downtown Marion.

The original parking lot on the south and west sides of the building provide 47 spaces. Street parking is available on three sides. As future growth makes enlarging the library necessary, 19 parking spaces will be lost. The old post office site across 11th Street has been acquired to provide about 50 future parking spaces.

The drive-up return on the Fifth Ave. side makes return of materials handy for library users.

Outside the south entrance, two bronze sculptures point to the virtues of young readers. Boy "Bookworm" is a gift from Suzanne and Bert Katz; girl "Bookworm II" (left rear) is a gift from the Murray family. Visiting children respond by talking to or touching the sculptures and trying to see what they are reading. Both sculptures are by Gary Lee Price.

City Square Entrance

The railroad theme is apparent in this close-up of the Sixth Ave. library entrance.

Inside, the lobby imitates a railroad station. Loaded book store carts invite browsers. At left, the library entryway and the kiosk that advertises coming events. Two other kiosks contain lists of fund contributors to the library and the Friends Library Foundation.

A Sculpture and Book Store

First Things Patrons See

University of Iowa professor of art Tom Aprile created the "TumbleRead" sculpture that was installed in the lobby in December 1996. The work embodies three primary ideas: essential symbols lauding strength of community, citizen literacy and growth and the city's long history as a hub of railroad activity.

Longtime volunteer Vern Haberkorn arranges books in the lobby outside the small store that has generated nearly $20,000 income annually. Quality donated merchandise is offered at reasonable prices with all profit going to the library for purchasing items not covered in the budget.

Book store volunteer Marj Reynolds, retired teacher, visits with customer, six-year-old Rebecca Darling. Miss Reynolds began working in the store when it opened in November 1996. The book store is open 36 hours per week, staffed by volunteers. Three managers have served: Marilyn Phelps, Mairi Mollman and, since 2003, Kay McGuire.

COLLECTIONS CATER TO AGE AND INTEREST GROUPS

The periodicals area features 279 magazines as well as nine different newspaper subscriptions. Retiree Bob Johnson, a regular library visitor since 1982, says the "fantastic new library" and "a very special staff" make progress possible with his two projects that require a "good bit of attention."

Young Adult area is arranged for teenage library patrons. Tables and chairs offer a comfortable area for perusing magazines and books of interest (at left). Countertop (at right) is standup work area for general reference books below.

Video collection of 8500 items includes more than 1500 in DVD format; the remainder in VHS format. Here patron Bruce Tompkins and his children Jonah, 4, and Josephine, 6, select videos to take home.

RESHELVING: A NEVER-ENDING TASK

Carts of returned books behind the checkout desk await re-shelving. At left, Dawn Martinez; Muriel Logan, at right.

Library page Ben Samuelson shelves returned books. The collection of some 122,388 books and other materials circulated 4.5 times in fiscal 2003-04. Materials include fiction and nonfiction books in print, cassette and CD format, video-cassettes and DVDs.

Magazine display area features nearly 300 publications. Current issues may be read in the library; back issues checked out for home reading. Here volunteer Michelle Penn returns borrowed magazines to their proper places ready for the next patrons.

LOWE MEETING ROOMS

More than 700 meetings took place in the library during fiscal 2003, averaging two each day the library was open. Library programs for citizens of all ages are popular. Preschool story times are scheduled each week along with summer and winter reading programs for adults, children and young adults.

The Lowe Meeting Rooms accommodate library staff and library-related meetings and numerous community organizations such as Linn County Extension, Cub and Boy Scouts, Grant Wood Area Education Association, both Marion school districts, investment clubs, men's and women's groups, City of Marion and Marion businesses that prefer to conduct meetings away from office interruptions. Above, an organization conducts a book exchange. The meeting area can be made into one room as it appears above, or divided into two rooms.

Multiple activities take place in the Library's meeting rooms. Check your interests.

____ **Book discussions**
____ **County extension**
____ **Crafting**
____ **Education**
____ **Investing**
____ **Library Friends meetings and programs**
____ **Scouting**
____ **Special library programs for children and young adults**
____ **Story times**

COMPUTERS FOR PATRONS AND STAFF

Computer keyboard—attended here by Ben Gustas and his grandmother, Eileen Robinson—enables patrons to search the electronic catalog and locate materials in the library. A search by author, subject or title is displayed on a monitor; the patron can either make note of the shelf location or have the retrieved information printed out.

Library computer use has tripled since 1996. In 1987, two Apple computers were used for cataloging and bookkeeping. In 2004, a total of 43 computers are used by staff and customers. Nine library Internet stations currently serve about 50 people daily to check e-mail, do research or search for jobs. One patron keeps in touch with her 100-year-old mother in Brazil via e-mail that is sent and received at the library.

Patrons can access a vast array of resources and databases in ten public catalogs that are Internet-based. Six other computers, programmed for patron word processing, reside in the information area.

Cubicles for staff in the work area of new library. Full-time staff members enjoy private work space with a computer. Here Chris Grannis, young adult librarian, works in her office area.

Six computers (above) in the library's Internet lab are connected to a reservation terminal activated by a patron card. A software system allows users to check themselves in and out of the lab, choose the computer they wish to use and request printout sheets of their work. Patrons pay for their copies; a staff member at the Information Desk releases jobs to the laser printer.

Reference librarian Judy Winistorfer assists a patron at the Information Desk. Queries by e-mail are invited.

CHECKING OUT

Handheld Wand Is State-of-the-Art

Come visit your library. Browse the shelves in the areas of your interest. Choose items you wish to take home. Each item is labeled with a barcode. The rubber stamp and card catalog of yesteryear have been replaced with the wand and an electronic catalog.

The staff member at the 'Check Out' desk will swipe the wand over the barcode on each item—and over your patron library card—to record borrower's name, item title, date borrowed and return date. You will be given a printed copy as a reminder.

The Marion Library is community-oriented. Staff members are helpful and pleasant. Think of us when you need reading, viewing and listening materials. When you seek information or need access to a computer, contact our Information Desk in person, by e-mail or telephone.

You will be in good company when you visit the Marion Library.

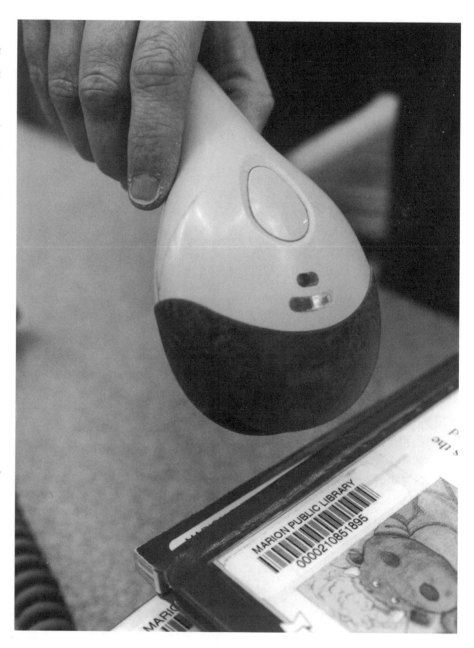

FRIENDLY STAFF AWAITS YOUR VISIT

Library Director Susan Kling has said she is blessed with an excellent staff. They are, left to right: (front) Sandy Ransier, Susan Kling, Cindi Brown, Kimberly Cowger; (second row) Becky Ramstad, Lynn Baumert, Julie Lammers, Marlene Aswegan; (third row) Chris Fee, Dawn Martinez, Muriel Logan, Roger Herrick, Lynn Strutton; (fourth row) Nancy Easley, Ben Samuelson, Pamela Walz, Jill Law, Jean Hampson, Jennifer Payne and Chris Grannis. Three staff members, at right, absent from the group photo, are (from left) Lara Moellers, Judy Winistorfer and Kathy Siegling.

Photos, Spring 2004

Appendices

•Library Board of Trustees

-1903 Library Board (First)

J.S. Alexander, President
E.I. Alderman
J.W. Bowman
Mrs. B.C. Busby
Miss Adeliza Daniels
Mrs. W.A. Dobson
Mrs. Bertha Owen
Gary Treat
Miss Emma Tyler

-1905 Board (Carnegie)

J.S. Alexander, President
E.I. Alderman
J.W. Bowman
Mrs. B.C. Busby
Mrs. W.A. Dobson
Mrs. Maude Marshall
Dr. James Moorhead
Mrs. Bertha Owen
Miss Emma Tyler

-1996 Board (new building)

Harry Baumert, President
Karen Andersen
Molly Andersen
Voanne Hansen
Irene Kincheloe
Reed Martin
John Messerli
Sally Reck
Eileen Robinson
Nancy A. Miller, ex officio

-Spring 2004 Board

Robert Buckley, President
Molly Andersen
Harry Baumert
Voanne Hansen
Irene Kincheloe
Sally Reck
Eileen Robinson
Linda Wilson
Jack Zumwalt
Nancy A. Miller, ex officio

•Library Board Members

[Due to incomplete records, we regret some names may be missing.]
Board member names and year first appointed since 1903.

Alderman E.I. 1903
Alexander J.S. 1903
Andersen Karen 1994
Andersen Molly 1974
Balster Llewellyn 1988
Baumert Harry 1989
Beeson Mabelle 1945
Blinks Leon 1934
Booth Dr. John 1928
Bouslog Jim 1991
Bowman James 1903
Bromwell James 1910
Buckley Robert 1997
Busby Cora 1903
Carson Vera 1939
Cessford Rose 1912
Daniels Adeliza 1903
DeWees Virginia 1974
Dobson Mrs. W.A. 1903
Donovan Blanche 1970
Engle Dan 1989
Ford Edwin H. 1956
Fowler John 1968
Frye Eugene 1963
Gertsen Kevin 2004
Glass George 1970
Goins Rev. Richard 1950
Gordon Hugh 1957
Granger Katherine 1937
Grayston Luzia 1923
Hansen Russell 1970
Hansen Voanne 1979
Hapgood Nancy 1982
Hastings D.D. 1959
Hay Marcella 1982
Hollingsworth Elmer 1926
Holmes Lloyd 1953
Howell Norma 1937
Kacena Kathy 1976
Kanak William 1971
Kellams Stanley 1939

Kellogg Jack 1976
Kemper Anita 1960
Kepros Steve 1978
Kincheloe Irene 1965
Kindervag Joyce 1972
King William 1974
Leidigh Dr. Roy 1939
Lensing Clair 1971
Mangold Julie 1975
Marshall Elizabeth 1909
Marshall Maude 1905
Martin Laurence 1979
Martin Reed 1995
Messerli John 1989
Millen Ella 1908
Miller Emery 1926
Miller Nancy A. 1994
Moorehead Dr. James 1905
Morgan Lowell 1982
Murdoch Faye 1953
Norris Linda 1976
Owen Bertha 1903
Oxley Marvin 1945
Parkhurst Louise 1908
Paul Margaret 1955
Reck Sally 1989
Reed Mary 1965
Riley Theresa 1970
Robinson Eileen 1988
Rose Dolores 1983
Ryan Miriam 1984
Schumack Frank 1916
Sieck Marlene 1971
Skinner Elizabeth 1928
Snell Hazel 1960
Strothman Jeanne 1977
Thayer Duane 1960
Treat Gary 1903
Tyler Emma 1903
White Martha 1950
Wilson Linda 1998
Wood W.E. 1907
Zumwalt Jack 2002

•Library Directors (9)

Nine different library directors have served the city and its citizens. Marion native Metta Whitcomb had the longest term of service. She was librarian for 27 years following nine years as apprentice and nine years as assistant to her predecessor, for a total of 45 years. Ruth Mills can be credited with bringing the Marion Library into the 20th Century, while present director, Susan Kling, ushered it into the 21st. By 2005 Susan Kling has been library director for 18 years. Bobbi Duss served 14 years and Lenna M. Huffman logged 13 years before her health gave out. During Miss Huffman's three-year illness, her assistant, Metta Whitcomb, ran the library for a $23-a-month salary. As economic conditions improved, Miss Whitcomb's salary had increased by 1955 to $130/mo.

1903–Mary Parkhurst, acting librarian for the first library, 2nd floor, across from City Park.
1905–1909, Mary Parkhurst, 4 years
1909–1912, Mabel Alexander, 3 years
1912–1919, Katherine Pierce, 7 years
1919–1932, Lenna M. Huffman, 14 years
1932–1959, Metta Whitcomb, 27 years
1959–1969, Ruth Mills, 10 years
1969–1983, Edith "Bobbi" Duss, 14 years
1983–1987, Gail Landy, 4 years
1987–Present, Susan Kling, 18 years.

•Children's Librarians (5)
Since 1957—
Alberta Marsh
Mary McCann
Anita Kemper
Leora Kriegermeier
Jean Hampson

•Library Staff, 2004 (24)
[Key: PT = Part time]
Susan Kling, Director
Cindi Brown, Assistant director
Chris Grannis, Young Adult librarian
Jean Hampson, Children's librarian
Jill Law, Circulation librarian
Judy Winistorfer, Reference librarian
Marlene Aswegan, PT Library Assisstant
Lynn Baumert, PT Library Clerk
Kimberly Cowger, PT Library Clerk
Nancy Easley, Library Assistant
Chris Fee, PT Library Assistant
Roger Herrick, permanent PT Library Page
Julie Lammers, permanent PT Library Assistant (story time)
Muriel Logan, PT Library Assistant
Dawn Martinez, Library Assistant
Lara Moellers, PT Library Page
Jennifer Payne, permanent PT Reference Assistant
Becky Ramstad, PT Library Assistant
Sandy Ransier, Library Assistant
Ben Samuelson, PT Library Page
Kathy Siegling, PT Library Assistant
Lynn Strutton, PT Library Assistant
Pamela Walz, permanent PT Library Administrative Assistant

•Marion Mayors (42)
[*Identifies men who served separate multiple terms]
Nov. 1865–March 1866, Thomas Jefferson McKean
March 1866–1867, Daniel Lothian
1868-1869, Thomas Corbett
1870, David Carskadden
1871–1874, *J.C. Davis
1875, D.T. McAfee
1876, J.C. Davis
1877, W.G. White
1878, Theodore P. Mentzer
1879, M.B. Allen
1880, March resignation, S.W. Rathbun
April 1880–December special election, B.F. Seaton
1881–1882, James D. Giffen
1883–1884, Alexander Campbell
1885–1886, D.L. Samson
1886–resignation Dec. 1889 J.C. Davis
Dec. 1889–1892, George B. Owen
March 1893–1894, John W. Dye,
1895–1898, *W.F. Fitzgerrald
Beginning in 1896, elections were held every two years.
1899–1903, P.M. Plumb
1903–1906, C.H. Marshall
1906 Nov.–April 1909, W. F. Fitzgerrald
1909 April–1913, Fergus L. Anderson
1913–1915, C.E. Gordon
1915–1919, C.A. Patten
1919–1923, C.W. Biggs
1923–1925, Dr. Arthur E. Crew
1925–1929, O.M. Carson
1929–1931, Dr. C.L. Drummond
1931–1933, O.M. Carson
1933–1941, John H. Pazour
1941–resigned August 1947, John C. Mullin
1947, Aug.–resigned Dec., 1953, M.H. Biddick
1954–resignation March 1955 (on sick leave much of the time), Elmer M. Seevell
1954, July–Dec. 23, 1954 (Acting

Mayor), C.R. Kisinger
1955, May–Jan. 1956, L.A. Franke
1956–Sept. 1963, George W. Brewer
1963, Sept.–November 1963,
 William R. Linstrom
1963, Nov.–Dec. 1968,
 Ralph W. Potter
1969, Jan.–Jan. 1970, Raymond
 Eckhart (Mayor Pro-tem)
1970, Jan.–Dec, 1971,
 Greg Hapgood
1972–1973, Chester W. Bullis
1974–1988, William J. Grundy, Jr.
1988–2003, Victor Klopfenstein
2004–Present, John Nieland

•City Managers (8)
February 1, 1964 to Present
02-01-64—11-31-68, Pete Crivaro
12-14-68—09-01-70, Don Wieh
09-14-70—03-15-73,
 Robert M.L. Johnson
12-06-73—05-10-74, Fred Day
06-20-74—07-01-76, Joe Painter
08-30-76—09-14-79, Larry Asaro
12-10-79—05-18-87, Carl Ramey
05-18-87—Present, Jeff Schott

•Postmasters (26)
Luman M. Strong, 1839-1844
Addison Daniels, 1844-1849
John Zumbro, 1849-1853
H.G. Welch, 1853-1860
William Downing, July 1, 1861–1865
T.S. Bardwell, 1865–1869, [1st to
 receive presidential appointment]
S.W. Rathbun, April 17,
 1869–Dec. 1880,
J.W. McClellan, Dec 1880–Jan. 1885
Norman E. Ives, May 1885-Jan. 1888
Joseph S. Lake, Feb 1888-Jan 1, 1891
Samuel Daniels, Jan 1891-Feb. 1895
Joseph Unangst, Feb 1895-May 1897
John S. Willard, May
 1897–Aug. 1900
E.I. Alderman, 1900–March 1902

Don Rathbun, March 1902–1910
J.S. Alexander, May 1910–1913
C.S. Shanklin, 1913–Sept
 17, 1916 (died)
T.T. (Thornt) Williams, May
 1916–Feb. 28, 1918 (died)
A.E. Granger, 1919–April 1936
Mary Mentzer Hollingsworth,
 April 1937–May 13, 1943 (died)
*[New post office on 8th
Ave. in 1938]*
Grace Koppenhaver,
 appointed to fill term
 of Hollingsworth
Charles Burns, Nov. 30, 1944
 –April 30, 1956 (resigned)
Leonard Brenneman, acting, May
1956-Sept. 21, 1956
 (resigned)
John Pazour, Sept. 22, 1956
 –Dec. 31, 1965 (retired)
Bernard "Spike" Mullaley,
 1966–Aug. 31, 1979 [New post
office 6th Ave. & 11th St. in 1969]
William Jackson, interim,
 Nov. 1979–Feb. 1980
Raymond A. Banowetz, Feb.
 9, 1980–Jan. 3, 1986 (retired)
Leonard Peck, acting, Jan.
 4, 1986 to Aug. 29, 1986
Cheryl Wernimont, Aug. 30,
 1986 to Feb. 1993, [Left to
 oversee 110 Iowa postal stations.]
Kim McCarty, Feb. 1993 to Present

•Marion Fire Chiefs (9)
All-volunteer firefighters
maintained safety before the
city took over in 1876 and began
mixing career personnel with
volunteers. One existing Mentzer
team uniform is treasured
by the Fire Department.

Elmer E. King, 1921-1935

Charles H. Sweet, 1936-1939
LeRoy Cooper, 1939-1942
 & 1947-1954
Edward Card, 1942-1947
Richard E. Cayler, 1954-1955
James H. Reynolds, 1955-1975
Vernon L. Blietz, 1976-1977
James L. Ford, 1977-1999
Terry S. Jackson, 1999-Present

•Marion Police Chiefs (12)
Before police, Marion had
town marshals. County sheriffs
maintained law and order before
the Marion Police Department
was established in 1936.
Gene Miller, 1936-1942 (resigned)
No police chief, 1943-44
Maurice Jacobs, 1945-1946
Michael Wachal, 1947-1948
Leighton Ford, 1948-1973
Richard Cayler, 1973-1977
Robert Zier, 1977-1984
Christopher Ebert, 1984-1986
Joe Neuhaus, Interim: Acting Chief
Mike Birmingham, 1987-Feb. 1991
Joe Neuhaus, Interim: Acting Chief
Mark Diamond, Nov.
 1991-Feb. 1996
Harry R. Daugherty, 1996-Present

•School Superintendents
Marion Independent Schools,
founded in 1860, was the fourth
school district in Iowa. Since 1971,
20 men have served. A website
provides additional information.
1871-1882, J.W. McClelland
1882-1884, D.N. Mason
1884-1890, E.J. Esgate
1890-1893, William Gemmill
1893-1901, J.J. Dofflemeyer
1902-1909, Grant Finch
1910-1911, F.L. Mahannah
1912-1920, O.M. Carson

1920-1921, L.R. Issacs
1921-1922, Paul Cutler
1922-1926, H.W. Chehock
1926-1956, Dr. C.B. Vernon
1956-1965, John Messerli
1965-1974, Dr. Richard Sorenson
1974-1977, Dr. Clark A. Stevens
1977-1979, Dr. C. Robert Bennett
1979-1986, Dr. Robert E. Hale
1986-1992, Dr. Harold Hulleman
1992-2003, Dr. William
  C. Jacobson
2003-Present, Nicholas Hobbs

•The Linn-Mar School District

was formed after 17 one-room rural
schools joined together in 1948.
By 2002, the district encompassed
64 square miles and included
the northern part of the city of
Marion, part of Cedar Rapids and
rural areas both north and south of
Marion. In recent years, the Linn-
Mar School District has been one
of the fastest growing in the state;
enrollment is expected to be steady
for the next few years. The district
maintains a website.
1948, T.C. Tibbets, Principal
1950, Harry Robson
  (Interim Principal)
1950, Clifford Wilkins, Principal
1959-1964, Clifford Wilkins, Supt.
1964-1966, James Bayne
1966-1971, Kenneth Patton
1971-1975, Dr. LeRoy Kruskop
1975-1993, Dr. Glen Easterday
1993-2003, Dr. Joseph Pacha
2003-Present, Dr. Katie Mulholland

•Marion Employers & Employees

The community has 65
manufacturing plants with
1,226 manufacturing employees.
Largest employers are listed:

-Product/Service, total employees
 2429
-Education, Linn-Mar 545
-Grocery store, Hy-Vee 300
-Telecommunications, US Cellular
 290
-Education, Marion Independent
 290
-Research, Consultation/Media,
 Magid Associates 185
-Government, City of Marion 136
-Financial institution, Farmers
 State Bank 134
-Food products machinery, Vector
 Corporation 101
-Mattresses, Lebeda Mfg. 90
-Agricultural and residential
 chemicals, Linn Cooperative Oil
 Co. 83
-Auto reconditioning & brake
 service, KW Products 80
-Fiberglass tub and showers,
 MAAX Midwest 61
-Livestock, animal feed, Wholesale
 Feeds 46
-Wholesale restaurant supplies,
 Rapids Wholesale 45
-Financial services, Berthel
 Fisher 43

•Marion Parks

The Marion Parks Department
maintains 18 parks, two ball fields,
one open area and Oak Shade
Cemetery. The parks in mid-2004
are:
Ascension Park
Boyson Park
Butterfield Park
City Park
Donnelly Park
Elza Park
Faulks Heritage Woods
Glenbrooke Cove
Hanna Park
Gill Park
Lininger Park
Lowe Park
Taube Park
Thomas Park
Legion Park
Tower Park
Willow Park
Willowood Park

Index

A Very Special Gift for family or friends!

You can purchase <u>The Marion Public Library: Doorway to the Future, Picture Window on the Past.</u>
at the Friends Bookstore in the Library ($15.00), or by mail from the library ($18.00).
For more information: Phone: 319-377-3412, or Email: mpl@mail.crlibrary.org

Prices include postage & handling. Checks only.

Please make checks payable to the *Friends of the Marion Library*

ORDER FORM

Enclosed please find check in the amount of $_____for _____ of copies of

<u>The Marion Public Library: Doorway to the Future, Picture Window on the Past.</u>

$18.00 each TOTAL $ _____

Send book(s) to: <u>Mail this order to:</u>

Name_____   Marion Public Library
                                                  1095 6th Ave.
Address_____   Marion, IA 52302

City_____State_____Zip_____